The Smithsonian Guides to Natural America
THE MID-ATLANTIC STATES

WA

The
Pacific
Northwest
OR

MT

The
Northern
Rockies

ND

The
Northern
Plains
SD

ID

WY

NE

NV

The
Far
West

CA

UT

The
Southern
Rockies

CO

KS

AZ

The
Southwest

NM

OK

TX

HI

The
Pacific

AK

The
Mid–Atlantic
States

Northern
New
England

ME

VT

NH

MA
CT RI

Southern
New
England

New York

New
Jersey

Pennsylvania

MN

WI

MI

The
Great
Lakes

IN

OH

MD
DE

IA

IL

The
Heartland

MO

WV

VA

The
Atlantic
Coast

KY

Central
Appalachia

TN

NC

The
South
Central
States

AR

MS

AL

GA

The
Southeast

SC

LA

FL

THE MID–ATLANTIC STATES
NEW YORK – PENNSYLVANIA
NEW JERSEY

THE SMITHSONIAN GUIDES
TO NATURAL AMERICA

THE MID-ATLANTIC STATES

NEW YORK, PENNSYLVANIA, AND NEW JERSEY

TEXT
Eugene Walter

PHOTOGRAPHY
Jonathan Wallen

PREFACE
Thomas E. Lovejoy

SMITHSONIAN BOOKS • WASHINGTON, D.C.
RANDOM HOUSE • NEW YORK, N.Y.

Front cover: Whiteface Mountain above Connery Pond, Adirondack Park
Half-title page: White-tailed deer
Frontispiece: Montauk Point, New York
Back cover: Hairy woodpecker; *Rhododendron maximum*; woodchuck

THE SMITHSONIAN INSTITUTION
SECRETARY I. Michael Heyman
COUNSELOR TO THE SECRETARY FOR
BIODIVERSITY AND ENVIRONMENTAL AFFAIRS Thomas E. Lovejoy
DIRECTOR, SMITHSONIAN PRESS/SMITHSONIAN PRODUCTIONS Daniel H. Goodwin
EDITOR, SMITHSONIAN BOOKS Alexis Doster III

THE SMITHSONIAN GUIDES TO NATURAL AMERICA
SERIES EDITOR Sandra Wilmot
MANAGING EDITOR Ellen Scordato
SERIES PHOTO EDITOR Mary Jenkins
ART DIRECTOR Mervyn Clay
ASSISTANT PHOTO EDITOR Ferris Cook
ASSISTANT PHOTO EDITOR Rebecca Williams
ASSISTANT EDITOR Seth Ginsberg
COPY EDITORS Helen Dunn, Karen Hammonds
FACT CHECKER Jean Cotterell
PRODUCTION DIRECTOR Katherine Rosenbloom

Library of Congress Cataloging-in-Publication Data
Walter, Eugene.
    The Smithsonian guides to natural America. The Mid-Atlantic States—
New York, Pennsylvania, New Jersey/text by Eugene Walter;
photography by Jonathan Wallen; preface by Thomas E. Lovejoy.
        p. cm.
    Includes bibliographical references (p. 260) and index.
    ISBN 0-679-76478-X (pbk.)
        1. Natural history—New York (State)—Guidebooks. 2. Natural
history—Pennsylvania—Guidebooks. 3. Natural history—New Jersey—
Guidebooks. 4. New York (State)—Guidebooks. 5. Pennsylvania—
Guidebooks. 6. New Jersey—Guidebooks I. Wallen, Jonathan.
II. Title.
    QH104.5.M45W35 1996   95-48074
    508.74—dc20   CIP
    Manufactured in the United States of America
    98765432

HOW TO USE THIS BOOK

The SMITHSONIAN GUIDES TO NATURAL AMERICA explore and celebrate the preserved and protected natural areas of this country that are open for the public to use and enjoy. From world-famous national parks to tiny local preserves, the places featured in these guides offer a splendid panoply of this nation's natural wonders.

Divided by state and region, this book offers suggested itineraries for travelers, briefly describing the high points of each preserve, refuge, park, or wilderness area along the way. Each site was chosen for a specific reason: Some are noted for their botanical, zoological, or geological significance, others simply for their exceptional scenic beauty.

Information pertaining to the area as a whole can be found in the introductory sections to the book and to each chapter. In addition, specialized maps at the beginning of each book and chapter highlight an area's geography and geological features as well as pinpoint the specific locales that the author describes.

For quick reference, places of interest are set in **boldface** type; those set in **boldface** followed by the symbol ❖ are listed in the Site Guide at the back of the book. (This feature begins on page 267, just before the index.) Here noteworthy sites are listed alphabetically by state, and each entry provides practical information that visitors need: telephone numbers, mailing addresses, and specific services available.

Addresses and telephone numbers of national, state, and local agencies and organizations are also listed. Also in appendices are a glossary of pertinent scientific terms and designations used to describe natural areas; the author's recommendations for further reading (both nonfiction and fiction); and a list of sources that can aid travelers planning a guided visit.

The words and images of these guides are meant to help both the active naturalist and the armchair traveler to appreciate more fully the environmental diversity and natural splendor of this country. To ensure a successful visit, always contact a site in advance to obtain detailed maps, updated information on hours and fees, and current weather conditions. Many areas maintain a fragile ecological balance. Remember that their continued vitality depends in part on responsible visitors who tread the land lightly.

CONTENTS

PREFACE

It has been 40 years since I first awakened to the wonders of natural America amid the imposing hills and rolling countryside of New York's Dutchess County. Just this week I experienced anew the vivid thrill of mid-Atlantic nature in the very same spot, on the verdant campus of the Millbrook School. There, red-winged blackbirds played sentinel in the marsh, tidy eastern kingbirds executed a changing of the guard at a nest, and a yellow warbler attempted to outdo Pavarotti, all against an auditory background of blackbirds' "scree" and the deep "glunk" of bullfrogs.

Not far away to the west at the Institute for Ecosystem Studies in Millbrook wild turkeys habitually visit a hilltop teahouse as if paying a matinal call, and to the east a stream rushes down a hidden Brigadoon of a valley named Turkey Hollow. A bit farther away near Bard College on the great Hudson River, I was initiated as a birdwatcher when a worm-eating warbler conveniently foraged upside down in the treetops, revealing the characteristic stripes of its crown.

New York, Pennsylvania, and New Jersey, the three states that constitute this portion of natural America, are rich in nature and in the history of natural science and conservation. In the north rise the Adirondacks, site of the largest park in the 48 contiguous states, where I climbed Mount Marcy and admired Lake Placid in the early 1950s. In Philadelphia, the garden of John Bartram, the great colonial botanist, can be visited, as can the Academy of Natural Sciences, the oldest continuously operating museum in the western hemisphere, which even preceded the Smithsonian.

Eastern Pennsylvania provides one of the great birding spots and early conservation victories at Hawk Mountain. Because of its convenient hot-air thermals, the ridge there becomes a critical funnel for birds of prey on their southward migration. Once the site of a stomach-turning annual slaughter (of so-called vermin), Hawk Mountain was preserved through the efforts of the redoubtable Rosalie Edge (who once made time for this

PRECEDING PAGES: *Near New York's Lake Champlain, an unspoiled landscape of marsh and russet hills lies at the eastern edge of Adirondack Park, the largest forest preserve in the contiguous United States.*

then-16-year-old passionate naturalist and conservationist at her tiny office on Lexington Avenue) and of initial curator Maurice Brown. Together they transformed the killing fields into a sanctuary. Now on a autumn day when the weather is right, a visitor can almost reach out and touch the magnificent birds as they float by.

Here, too, in midtown Manhattan, I helped return peregrine falcons to an urban environment atop the Metropolitan Life Insurance Building. Today a breeding pair nests behind the giant letters marking the Met Life building next to Grand Central Station. (The last ones in the city had nested outside the suite of Olivia de Haviland in the Saint Regis Hotel.) The recovery of the peregrine after DDT was phased out is one of the real environmental success stories.

ABOVE: *A red-shouldered hawk hunts from its perch on a tree bough. This common eastern resident prefers to spot prey while still, rather than from the air.*

The glaciers have left their imprint on the Mid-Atlantic with a legacy of lakes, sandy soils, and till. Long Island is actually the terminal moraine of one of the great glaciers. On the Atlantic side, Fire Island parallels part of the Long Island coastline and offers more than sand and sun. A visitor can enjoy expeditions to the oasis of the Sunken Forest and can find brilliant scarlet sponges and other marine life growing on the piers.

North of New York City—which despite its urban exuberance has never managed to overwhelm the nearby Palisades—the Hudson Highlands continue to provide the same inspiration that so heavily influenced Thomas Cole, Asher Durand, and Frederic Edwin Church of the Hudson River School, artists whose works are so well represented in the Smithsonian's National Museum of American Art. Beyond the Hudson to the west, the purplish blue of the Catskills ornament the horizon. Cool hemlock-dominated gorges such as Mianus and "sky lakes" carved by glaciers into ridgetops sprinkle the region.

Notwithstanding impressions to the contrary, the Mid-Atlantic harbors

abundant wild areas. New Jersey has the Delaware Water Gap and the spectacular Pine Barrens, home of the natty carpenter frog and the endangered Pine Barrens frog. New York glories in Niagara and two Great Lakes, all the Finger Lakes, Lake Champlain and crystalline Lake George, so exciting for swimming or canoeing across (if the weather held) when I was a boy. New England may think it holds the edge on autumn color, but the Mid-Atlantic gives it a good run for its money. Near Erie, Pennsylvania, Presque Isle boasts 500 species of flowering plants and ferns. New Jersey's Cape May is a mecca for birdwatchers waiting for propitious weather to generate fallouts, when enormous numbers of migrants suddenly put down to await better traveling conditions. And the city of Philadelphia contains the Tinicum marsh, which I am delighted is now a national wildlife refuge named in honor of my treasured friend, the great Pennsylvania environmentalist and senator John Heinz.

It was here near the Schuylkill River that an illiterate eighteenth-century farmer, John Bartram, paused while plowing one day and looked, as he had never looked before, at a flower. Totally transformed, Bartram went on to develop such an enormous passion for botany that he not only learned to read but also mastered Latin as well, a requisite for botanists of the time. How he became Royal Botanist for the colonies (George III and Queen Charlotte had an interest in the subject) is a story in itself. More important, however, is that the same potential for transformation is in each of us if only we'd pause to really look at nature. Bartram's epiphany happened in Pennsylvania. Indeed, it can happen anywhere. But the Mid-Atlantic is a great place to begin.

—Thomas E. Lovejoy
Counselor to the Secretary for
Biodiversity and Environmental Affairs,
SMITHSONIAN INSTITUTION

LEFT: *Autumn leaves carpet a walkway along the Gorge Trail in Watkins Glen, New York. Fine sand swept along in the river's current created the gorge's terraced chutes; at water level the rock has been polished smooth.*

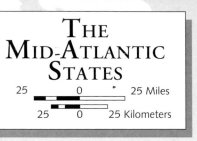

THE
MID-ATLANTIC
STATES

| 25 | 0 | * | 25 Miles |

| 25 | 0 | 25 Kilometers |

Lake   Ontario

Rochester

CANADA

Buffalo

NEW

Lake Erie

Erie

ALLEGHENY PLATEAU

OHIO

PENNSYLVANIA

Pittsburgh

VALLEY AND RIDGE PROVINCE

HARRISBURG

MARYLAND

WEST VIRGINIA

INTRODUCTION

INTRODUCTION:

THE MID-ATLANTIC STATES

Nature in the Mid-Atlantic region of the United States strikes many people, residents included, as an oxymoron. After all, New York, Pennsylvania, and New Jersey are part of the Northeastern Corridor Megalopolis. This most densely populated piece of the country is anchored by America's largest city, as well as other metropolises where the human census runs into hundreds of thousands, sometimes even millions. Yet the oxymoronic view that sees only overcrowded cities and highways clogged with traffic is a glass-is-half-empty perspective. The glass-is-half-full characterization is closer to the truth. Although no detailed photographs chronicle the region as it appeared two or three centuries ago, records do exist in the romantic, bucolic scenes painted by such artists of the Hudson River School (1825–75) as Thomas Cole, Asher Durand, and Frederic Edwin Church. Their images of the Hudson River countryside, the Catskill Mountains, the Adirondacks, the Finger Lakes, the Delaware Water Gap, and Niagara Falls are documentaries of an unsullied Mid-Atlantic region. Amazingly, most locations remain recognizable.

In this area today forests, even large ones, are tranquil and smog-free, many still populated not only by the ubiquitous white-tailed deer but also by black bears, beavers, otters, bobcat, and more. Come spring, trilliums, violets, and lady's slippers illuminate woodland shadows; warblers, tanagers, and vireos decked out in flashy breeding plumage still flit from branch to branch seizing juicy caterpillars, and ovenbirds call "Teacher! Teacher! Teacher!" In wetland pools, painted turtles continue to line up like armored soldiers to sun themselves atop fallen trees, and at twilight, spring peepers announce their froggy mating intentions with the same high-pitched intensity that has characterized them for generations. Wild rivers persist, patrolled by swift ospreys and bald eagles.

PRECEDING PAGES: *Edged by golden phragmites (a reed), a boardwalk crosses a seaside marsh in New Jersey's Cape May Point State Park. Massive flocks of birds migrate through this area in spring and fall.*

4

Crystalline creeks surge between boulder-strewn banks draped with mosses and ferns. And waterfalls have not ceased to leap down rocky precipices; hundreds take the plunge.

Even virgin forests have survived in this crowded part of the world—trees 300 or 400 years old that were alive when European settlers arrived. These pristine parcels, however, are measured in square yards, not square miles. Broadly speaking, nature has endured in New York, Pennsylvania, and New Jersey in little islands in an urban/industrial sea, not in million-acre expanses protected as preserves and parks.

These few natural remnants survive because someone had the foresight to protect them or because their location happened to shield them. Some timber groves were not logged because they grew on terrain too steep or too boggy to make cutting safe and economically feasible. Thanks to nineteenth-century land surveys, which were not as precise as today's, landowners often left plots of trees rather than risk harvesting a neighbor's property.

Much Mid-Atlantic space can be classified as recovered, reclaimed, revived, or restored—in effect, "used nature." The majority of forests are second growth—logged and allowed to reseed and grow to maturity. As agriculture declined in the region and farms failed, fields reverted to a wild state. During the twentieth century an aroused citizenry began to realize that the area's natural heritage was disappearing. Occasionally, dedicated souls removed scars left by developers and restored the landscape to a semblance of its original grandeur. New laws and regulations set aside preserves, cleaned up water and air, and designated protected status for much of the wild flora and fauna. Besides federal rankings, each of the Mid-Atlantic states has devised its own lists of endangered species.

Our forebears diminished the diversity of wildlife significantly, eradicating, for example, predators such as wolves and cougars from the region. Millions of passenger pigeons passing overhead blotted sun and sky from view until market hunters rendered the species extinct in 1914. Bison, which formerly ranged as far east as New York, were earlier casualties. Once plentiful in Mid-Atlantic forests, elk and moose were hunted out of existence. Birds of prey were gunned from the sky with abandon because of the misguided notion that they were "bad." Victims of their own luxurious fur, beavers were trapped almost to the point of no return.

Although hunting has done substantial harm, even more damage has been caused by the elimination of wild habitat. Migratory songbird pop-

ABOVE: *New York artist Jasper Francis Cropsey painted* Autumn on the Hudson River *in 1860. When the work was exhibited in London, the vivid*

ulations, for instance, have declined because of forest fragmentation (by roads, power lines, real estate development) in the Mid-Atlantic region. Today wildlife is often restricted to creatures that coexist easily with people. Raccoon, opossums, and skunks make homeowners apoplectic by raiding garbage cans and carrying the threat of rabies; deer with no predators—unless automobiles count—to hold their numbers to normal levels overpopulate and devour gardens; and Canada geese, provided

foliage astounded English viewers. Cropsey had to produce real fall leaves from the Hudson Valley to demonstrate his fidelity to nature.

with golf courses and lawns to feed on, no longer migrate and make a mess of suburban neighborhoods.

Although not as lush as it was 300 years ago, the region's inventory of wildlife is still rich and slowly improving. Left alone, beavers staged a comeback. Moose have begun returning to northern New York, and the state of Pennsylvania has reintroduced elk. A black bear population is booming in northwestern New Jersey's Kittatinny Mountains and

ABOVE: *A bull elk drinks from a stream. In warm weather, elk graze in mountain pastures; they descend to woodlands as winter approaches.*

Pennsylvania's Poconos. Wolves are probably gone for good, but coyotes have moved in. Although raptors such as bald eagles, peregrine falcons, and ospreys were devastated by DDT and other pesticides—they ceased to breed in most of the Mid-Atlantic region—new regulations curtailed the use of such poisons. Through captive breeding programs and special release techniques, state conservation agencies have helped raptors to rebound and repopulate areas where they had vanished. Migratory songbird populations have dwindled, but the good news is that there are still millions—only a half-dozen species are endangered. In fact, the Mid-Atlantic states, in the heart of an alley of migration, boast some of the most spectacular birding hot spots in all North America.

Nature in the Mid-Atlantic area may survive in fragments, and it may be "used"—abused in many cases—but it is basically healthy. The battle to keep it that way will probably never end. Contrary to the oxymoronic image, there is *much* nature to enjoy here; the glass is *more* than half full.

RIGHT: *Red maples thrive in the Delaware Water Gap National Recreation Area, which flanks the Delaware in Pennsylvania and New Jersey.*

NEW YORK

PART ONE

N E W   Y O R K

New York seems a lot larger than it is. At 49,576 square miles, it ranks 30th out of America's 50, but it packs a lot within its borders. New York is a place of superlatives, encompassing some of the most spectacular beaches on the East Coast, world-class wildlife refuges, beautiful river valleys immortalized by renowned American artists, the Adirondacks (the largest park in the country outside Alaska), two Great Lakes, and one of the world's grandest cataracts, Niagara Falls.

Amid such natural splendors live nearly 18 million people, almost half of them in five big cities, including America's largest metropolis, New York City. The state is a center of industry, commerce, and agriculture—number one in cream and cottage cheese, the country's third largest producer of milk, and a national leader in sweet corn, onions, and apples. The Big Apple is the nation's financial capital—dominant in banking, the securities trade, and communications—and one of the country's busiest transportation hubs.

Who would have predicted such riches four centuries ago? Certainly not Giovanni da Verrazano, who, sailing for the French, dropped anchor around New York Harbor in 1524, the first European to do so. He made no claim, but in 1609 English explorer Henry Hudson navigated his namesake river, claiming it and the surrounding area for the Dutch. Eventually the colony of New Netherland, founded in 1624, encompassed both New York and New Jersey. The first governor, Peter Minuit, negotiated one of history's greatest land swindles in 1626 when he purchased Manhattan Island from the native Canarsie people for trinkets worth about $24.

The Dutch ruled until 1664, when they surrendered the colony to the British, who split New Netherland into two parts, renaming the larger portion New York after the Duke of York. Commerce thrived for another century. During the Revolution, New York occupied such a strategic position that nearly one third of the war's battles were fought here. Under the fledgling republic, opportunities for new industries and transportation exploded. A network of barge canals linked the Great Lakes—and thus the Midwest—with the Hudson River and New York City. The label Empire State was coined.

PRECEDING PAGES: *Lower Saranac Lake lies in the heart of the Adirondacks. A century ago its pure air made Saranac a celebrated health resort.*

Today New York encompasses the most extensive natural areas of any eastern state, and over two centuries it has pioneered standards now followed by all the states. Niagara Reservation, with its fabulous falls, was designated America's first state park in 1885. The same year state legislators established the Adirondack and Catskills forest preserves, which later also became state parks. Its more than six million acres make Adirondack the biggest park of any kind in the lower 48 states; only a couple of national parks in Alaska are larger. The Catskill Park is a mere ten percent of Adirondack, but 600,000 acres are nothing to sneeze at. Today the state contains upward of 200 parks and historic sites that attract more than 50 million visitors annually. In addition, many localities own splendid, little-known parks that are natural marvels, not just picnic grounds and ball fields. Suffolk County, on eastern Long Island, for instance, boasts several gems.

Although largely uncelebrated, New York's state forests are a significant natural treasure. Since the 1920s the state has acquired more than 850,000 acres—mostly impoverished and abandoned farmland—for reforestation. Today approximately 400 state forests vary greatly in size, many taking jagged shapes and some fragmented into two or more tracts. Although a number lack recreation facilities, others offer peaceful woodland trails for hiking as well as excellent birding opportunities. Morgan Hill State Forest near Apulia Station, for example, occupies a 5,000-acre plateau blanketed in northern hardwood trees and conifers and cut by a creek that plummets over a 50-foot waterfall. Exquisite in autumn, Morgan Hill, like virtually all the state forests, is patronized almost exclusively by local people. Such less-crowded natural sites, however, are worth seeking.

Unlike the vast holdings that the federal government administers in the West, there are no national parks within New York—although Fire Island National Seashore and Gateway National Recreation Area, managed by the National Park Service, come close. The U.S. government oversees one small national forest outside Ithaca and a handful of national wildlife refuges, most located on Long Island. In addition, the Nature Conservancy, a private organization, has preserved an abundance of precious sites from the Adirondacks to Long Island and western New York; many of them can also be visited.

With its whopping human population, multifarious industries, and thriving agriculture, New York is a place of unparalleled diversity. Visitors soon discover that variety is also the rule in its parks and preserves. From pristine beaches to craggy mountains, from wooded gorges to cascading waterfalls, New York remains a state of uncommon natural wonders.

13

CHAPTER ONE

SOUTHERN NEW YORK:
NEW YORK CITY, LONG ISLAND, AND THE LOWER HUDSON VALLEY

T raveling north along one of the country roads that parallel the Hudson River in late summer and early fall, visitors find woodlands, meadows, and roadside shoulders bright with black-eyed Susans, purple New England asters, and sprays of goldenrod. The natural scene alternates with carefully tended farmlands: pastures where dairy cattle feed; apple orchards where ripe fruit bends the branches; and fields where tall stalks of corn await harvest. Eventually the road weaves through small, picturesque mountains, and the farther north it stretches, the wilder and more interesting the landscape becomes to nature lovers. Here visitors can still enjoy the kind of scenery that inspired the nineteenth-century artists of the Hudson River School.

The river's southern terminus is swallowed by the colossus of New York City—chockablock with humanity, automobiles, and high-rise buildings—where nature can seem almost an alien presence. Many inhabitants would probably concur with filmmaker Woody Allen, who once described himself as "at two with nature." Yet even the most indifferent urbanites flock to the tokens of nature embodied in the greensward of parks and in the sand and surf of nearby beaches.

The Hudson River is the chain that links the extremes of natural north and urban south. After beginning life as a wetland trickle in the Adirondack Mountains, the river widens and deepens as it flows to-

LEFT: *The setting sun burnishes a pebbled beach at Smith Cove in Shelter Island's Mashomack Preserve. Before English colonists arrived, Shinnecock and Montauk peoples hunted and fished along this shoreline.*

LEFT: *In Asher B. Durand's 1849* **Kindred Spirits,** *Hudson River School painter Thomas Cole (right) and poet William Cullen Bryant admire an idyllic vista. Bryant saluted the hills as "rock-ribbed, and ancient as the sun."*

ward New York City. Just north of Manhattan, it spreads out as the Tappan Zee, a name Dutch settlers gave this stretch because it reminded them of an inland sea. In its most scenic moments, the Hudson is walled by sheer cliffs such as the Hudson Highlands, and closer to Gotham, the Palisades.

Daily tides and salt water from the Atlantic Ocean reach up the lower Hudson all the way to Troy, about 160 miles from the coast. Thus the waterway fooled explorer Henry Hudson into believing—briefly—that he had found a northwest passage across an uncharted land.

Towns and industries along the river have abused it, often treating the waters like a convenient sewer. In the latter part of the twentieth century, conservation and cleanup efforts have begun to restore a semblance of riverine respectability. Fish populations are recovering. Even in its most depressing, polluted moments, the Hudson never ceased to be a major highway for migrating birds—lots of them.

A surprising number of natural delights have survived the clutter of civilization in this megalopolitan region. To explore them, the itinerary for the chapter begins in Manhattan, travels to the eastern end of Long Island, and then heads up the Hudson River to a triad of small, enchanting mountain ranges, each with a distinctly different character.

METROPOLITAN NEW YORK AND LONG ISLAND

Manhattan's heavily used **Central Park**❖ is seminatural, a landscaped, mostly artificial plot designed in the mid-1800s by Frederick Law Olmsted and Calvert Vaux to embody a romantic image of nature. To a

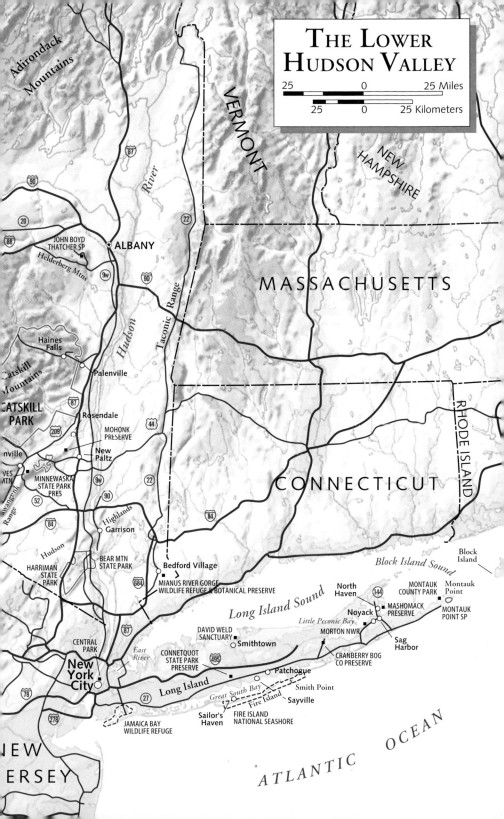

THE LOWER
HUDSON VALLEY

25   0   25 Miles
25   0   25 Kilometers

Adirondack Mountains

VERMONT

NEW HAMPSHIRE

20

88

JOHN BOYD
THATCHER SP

Helderberg Mtns

★ ALBANY

90

9W

90

River

Hudson

Taconic Range

MASSACHUSETTS

Haines
Falls

Catskill Mountains

CATSKILL
PARK

87

Palenville

Rosendale

209

MOHONK
PRESERVE

44

nville

New Paltz

VES
TN

MINNEWASKA
STATE PARK
PRES

9W

22

awangunk
Range

52

90

CONNECTICUT

RHODE ISLAND

84

Highlands

Garrison

84

Hudson

HARRIMAN
STATE
PARK

BEAR MTN
STATE PARK

Bedford Village

684

MIANUS RIVER GORGE
WILDLIFE REFUGE & BOTANICAL PRESERVE

Block Island Sound

Block
Island

North
Haven

144

MONTAUK
COUNTY PARK

Montauk
Point

MONTAUK
POINT SP

Noyack

MASHOMACK
PRESERVE

Long Island Sound

Little Peconic Bay

MORTON NWR

Sag
Harbor

87

CENTRAL
PARK

*East
River*

DAVID WELD
SANCTUARY

Smithtown

CONNETQUOT
STATE PARK
PRESERVE

495

CRANBERRY BOG
CO PRESERVE

New
York
City

Patchogue

78

Long Island

27

Great South Bay

Fire Island

Smith Point

Sayville

Sailor's
Haven

FIRE ISLAND
NATIONAL SEASHORE

278

JAMAICA BAY
WILDLIFE REFUGE

NEW
JERSEY

ATLANTIC OCEAN

ABOVE: *With New York City's World Trade Center looming in the distance, snow geese and dark-plumaged brant congregate in West Pond at Jamaica Bay Wildlife Refuge, a stopover for many migrating waterfowl.*

bird flying above on a seasonal migratory journey, these 843 acres shine like a heaven-sent green oasis in a vast wasteland of steel and concrete. About 265 species have been recorded in the park, including roughly 35 warbler species, predominantly songbirds passing through from March 1 through June 7 (peak numbers occur in May). Some 140 to 150 species alight at various times during this period, and the numbers in September and October are only slightly lower.

Across the East River from Manhattan, two other boroughs, Brooklyn and Queens, occupy the western end of Long Island. In Queens on the west side of Cross Bay Boulevard, 1.5 miles south of the North Channel Bridge, is the city's premier birding hot spot, **Jamaica Bay Wildlife Refuge❖.** A division of the **Gateway National Recreation Area,** the refuge is accessible by car as well as public transportation (subway or bus and a short walk). Until the 1950s the area was a watery wasteland of tidal marsh, mudflats, and bay where wildlife was sparse. A program of filling in land, dredging ponds, and planting trees, shrubs, grasses,

ABOVE: *Among the many species plying the Atlantic Flyway and visiting Jamaica Bay are double-crested cormorants (top), glossy ibis (bottom left), and mute swans (bottom right), which may have cygnets in tow.*

and flowering plants transformed the raw materials into habitats hospitable to a broad spectrum of wildlife. Now the 9,155-acre refuge combines salt marsh, ponds of fresh and brackish water, upland fields and woodlands, and the broad expanse of bay and islands.

Not only is the sanctuary within sight of one of America's busiest airports (John F. Kennedy International) and rimmed by parkways, it is also at a major crossroads for migratory birds: the intersection of the Atlantic Flyway and the Hudson River. Habitat upgrade has enabled the refuge to record 329 bird species: shorebirds, waders, waterfowl, gulls, terns, birds of prey, songbirds. Thousands stop on spring and fall migrations, and at least 60 species nest here. Also present in warm weather are great bevies of butterflies (more than 50 species), and special areas are managed to encourage their presence.

Long Island is a glacial garbage dump of stone, gravel, and sand known as a moraine, augmented over 10,000 years by tons of ocean sand courtesy of sea currents and waves. Poking eastward 125 miles

19

into the Atlantic like a separated finger, it is part of the coastal plain that extends along much of the eastern seaboard. Beyond Brooklyn and Queens at the western end, most of the island (Nassau and Suffolk counties) is covered by housing developments, shopping malls, and corporate parks. Tucked into suburbia, however, are numerous state and county parks, national wildlife refuges, and Nature Conservancy preserves where visitors may indulge an interest in birds or botany.

The wildest place is Fire Island, which lies off the south shore across Great South Bay (reached May through November by ferries from Patchogue, Sayville, and Bay Shore and all year by the Robert Moses Causeway and the Smith Point Bridge.) A barrier island that absorbs the buffeting of the Atlantic's wind and waves, Fire Island measures 32 miles long, little more than half a mile wide, and 30 feet at its highest altitude. Although New Yorkers consider its 18 cottage communities great places to rent summer houses, more than half of the island is protected in its natural state as **Fire Island National Seashore❖;** its western tip is preserved as **Robert Moses State Park.**

Flat, sweeping stretches of blinding white-sand beaches ripple into wind-blown dunes that mimic the waves washing Fire Island's coast. Within that context are other ecological pockets: parched, grassy swales, woodsy thickets, mudflats, maritime forests, freshwater bogs, and salt marshes. West of Sailor's Haven, a series of dunes rise 30 feet, supporting on their lee side (away from ocean and wind) a fairy-tale woodland called the **Sunken Forest.** The grainy "mountains" block the murderous salt spray, allowing the forest to survive, albeit in miniature. A leafy canopy of shadbush, American holly, red maples, red oaks, sassafras, and tupelo creates a gnarly frame for clinging tendrils of wild grapes, catbriers, and poison ivy.

Between Watch Hill and Smith Point, a seven-mile segment of the island is the only federally designated wilderness in New York State. A hike in spring or fall, when human traffic is scarce, can be otherworldly. Simultaneously warmed by the sun and cooled by sea breezes, visitors scrunch over shifting sands past groves of twisty pines and

RIGHT: *At Fire Island's Robert Moses State Park, wind-whipped dune grass seems ablaze in the late afternoon sun. The lighthouse stands sentinel over Great South Bay, threatened by pollution and development.*

LEFT: *A solitary willet forages on the beach at Fire Island as the evening tide rolls in. In the fall, the willets move south, leaving the wave-swept Long Island shoreline to hardier species such as eiders, harlequin ducks, and purple sandpipers.*

RIGHT: *A female Forster's tern accepts a morsel of fish from her attentive mate. Only in breeding season do the birds develop black caps; in the winter, the head marking fades to a black band behind the eye. They breed in marshy areas.*

marshy hollows. Their only companions are shorebirds stutter-stepping through sand and surf and rafts of ducks bobbing over waves offshore. All around, birdcalls, wind, and water harmonize in soothing sound. The experience is like a visit to the island 400 years ago—before real estate agents arrived.

Back on the mainland at **Connetquot River State Park Preserve**❖ (off Route 27 in Oakdale), the pure, unpolluted river flows amid 3,500 acres of hardwood forests, pine barrens, and woodland swamps. A favorite destination of Long Island birders, the park is a haven for waterfowl, owls, hawks, ospreys, and countless songbirds. A permit is required to visit. On the island's north shore outside Nissequogue the **David Weld Sanctuary**❖, a Nature Conservancy preserve, stretches inland from 1,800 feet of beach and bluffs fronting Long Island Sound. A diverse assembly of trees, shrubs, vines, wildflowers, and ferns flourishes in northern hardwood forest, wooded swamp, a kettle-hole community, and an overgrown field. Take Moriches Road north to Horse Race Lane, turn right, go .4 miles, and bear left onto Boney Lane.

The **Cranberry Bog County Preserve**❖, on East Moriches-Riverhead Road (Route 51), is a relic of the the time when Suffolk County was America's third largest cranberry producer. Now a county preserve, the bog supports a rich community of plants, among them two kinds of cranberries and other heaths such as leatherleaf, swamp honeysuckle, and blueberry, plus 13 orchid species, many of them rare.

At the eastern end of Long Island near the village of Noyack, the **Morton National Wildlife Refuge**❖ is one of nine preserves in the

Long Island National Wildlife Refuge Complex. (At Exit 9 of the Sunrise Highway, or Route 27, take Route 38 or North Sea/Noyack Road north for five miles to the refuge entrance.) The 187-acre preserve occupies a long fingerlike peninsula that separates Little Peconic and Noyack bays. In these salty, sheltered waters live aquatic turtles such as loggerheads, ridleys, and diamondback terrapins. Sand, gravel, and rock beaches surround the peninsula, and a self-guided nature trail wanders through its upland forest and open fields, visiting brackish and freshwater ponds and the salt marsh and lagoon. Morton provides protected habitat for native deer and red foxes and a variety of birds—nesting ospreys, double-crested cormorants, least terns—as well as quail, roseate terns, scoters, oldsquaw, and endangered piping plover. Generations of tame black-capped chickadees have been feeding on sunflower seeds from the hands of visitors for more than 40 years.

Several miles farther east in nearby Sag Harbor, ferry service on Route 114 in North Haven transports visitors to **Shelter Island.** The entire southeastern corner (2,039 acres) of the island is the Nature Conservancy's **Mashomack Preserve❖** on Gardiners Bay. Behind 10

In an 1829 Audubon painting (above), an osprey grasps a weakfish in its strong talons. Many of these formidable raptors breed in the Mashomack Preserve (left), where Miss Annie's Creek flows placidly to Smith Cove and Gardiners Bay.

miles of white-sand shore, 17 miles of trails explore a medley of maritime ecosystems: tidal creeks, salt marshes, 1,400 acres of oak and beech forest plus other woodlands, and open fields. The most notable habitat is a pine swamp complex where all the vegetation is rooted in a floating sphagnum moss mat ten feet thick in places. Feathery water willows ring the swamp, lightly shading such shrubs as highbush blueberry, winterberry, mountain holly, and swamp azalea. Beneath a dense grove of white pines rising from the heart of the sphagnum, rare orchids bloom in spring.

Some 82 bird species nest in this wildlife-friendly environment. When spring comes, pairs of ospreys return from South American winter haunts. In the colony of these large raptors at Mashomack, one of the densest in the Northeast, ospreys build bulky nests of sticks and dried seaweed in snags along the coast and in the salt marshes. Wings beating

OVERLEAF: *On a crystal clear morning, the Atlantic Ocean laps at Montauk's rocky perimeter. In the 1700s, whales abounded here, often washing ashore; today, the great leviathans can be spotted only at sea.*

furiously, an osprey parent hovers over water to get a bead on a fish dinner. The bird plunges in feet-first, then explodes upward, its talons clutching an unlucky victim. After circling proudly with the writhing fish, it heads home to feed the family. Ospreys are hard to beat for drama.

On the easternmost tip of Long Island's south fork, at the very end of Montauk Highway, lies Montauk Point. On the north side near Shagwong Point **Montauk County Park❖** encloses nearly 1,100 acres of shaded hardwood forest, fecund salt marsh and swamplands, and a rocky, sandy beach that stretches along Block Island Sound. The focus is Big Reed Pond, a 53-acre national natural landmark; despite its short distance from the ocean, this freshwater pond is fed by springs.

Montauk Point State Park❖ to the southeast is land's end. Here dense woodlands are home to abundant wildlife, including deer, raccoon, woodchucks, and foxes. The very tip of Long Island near historic Montauk Lighthouse affords spectacular views of the Atlantic Ocean and Block Island Sound. During autumn and winter, visitors with binoculars can spot seabirds that come close to land only late in the year. They may also see sleek harbor seals, which often haul out on offshore rocks. And for the seaworthy, whale-watching tours are available nearby.

UP THE RIVER

North of New York City in upper Westchester County one can explore a landmark sanctuary. The **Mianus River Gorge Wildlife Refuge and Botanical Preserve❖,** off Miller's Mill Road a short drive east of the green in Bedford Village, is the Nature Conservancy's very first project. In a deep ravine, the river has created a cool, moist microclimate that fosters a botanical assembly typical of regions farther north. A trail wanders through climax forest of oak, beech, black birch, and hemlock that contains some 300-year-old virgin trees. Although the path follows the river only briefly, it frequently affords vistas of the whitewater stream and the big splash of Havermeyer Falls. The preserve protects 55 acres of confirmed old-growth forest along 2.5 miles of river.

RIGHT: *The majestic Hudson River curves north at West Point toward the massive bulk of Storm King Mountain. The river achieves its greatest depth along this stretch, which is popularly known as World's End.*

Several counties in this neighborhood sit atop bedrock forged more than a billion years ago when a variety of even older rocks, subjected to monumental heat and pressure within the earth, metamorphosed into a completely different type of rock. Eventually the mass cooled into a rocky complex, most of which was an extremely hard, coarse-grained pinkish-gray stone called granitic gneiss. Although sturdy, this gneiss is no match for the Hudson River and its glacial allies. Millions of years later, river and ice carved a narrow gorge 15 miles long through the rock, leaving steep cliffs rising like ramparts to flank both shores from Peekskill north to Newburgh—the Hudson Highlands.

At the southern end, two state parks—**Bear Mountain**❖ and then **Harriman**❖—perch above the west bank of the river. They share a common border, making one large swath of preserved land that covers 51,680 acres. A short drive from the park entrance on Route 9W, Bear Mountain's summit glows pale pink from its expanse of exposed bedrock. Although the elevation is only 1,305 feet, Perkins Memorial

Shawangunks, Catskills, and Helderbergs

LEFT: *A sweeping view north from Bear Mountain Bridge encompasses fecund marshes, heavily wooded highlands, and the Hudson itself. The river carved a deep, narrow channel through these ancient hills about ten million years ago as it rampaged south to the Atlantic Ocean from its headwaters in the Adirondacks.*

Tower at the mountain's pinnacle provides panoramic views of the countryside that extend many miles up, down, and across the river. Four states can be seen: New York, New Jersey, Connecticut, and Pennsylvania. From late August into November, it's a prime spot for hawk-watching.

Forests cover about 90 percent of the parklands—Harriman is the wilder of the two—giving them a primeval look even though they have been cut several times. Browsing by an overpopulation of deer has rendered these woodlands remarkably free of underbrush and young trees. Within forest precincts lie 26 lakes, numerous mountain brooks, and a variety of marshes, swamps, bogs, and open meadows connected by hundreds of miles of trails. More than 250 bird species have been recorded in this area; 100 of them nest here. Woodpeckers are plentiful, and from spring until fall there is a wealth of wood warblers.

SHAWANGUNKS, CATSKILLS, AND HELDERBERGS

Northwest of the Hudson Highlands, three groups of mountains huddle together in scenic neighborliness. The Shawangunk (pronounced shawn-gum) range is a more-or-less flattop ridge, an eastern finger of the Valley and Ridge Province that runs along the edge of the Allegheny Plateau about 50 miles from Rosendale to the New Jersey border. The tabletop is composed of conglomerate, a sedimentary rock formed along inland seas about 420 million years ago when trillions of quartz pebbles were embedded in a cementlike batter of sand. Polished by water for eons, the quartz imparts a white sheen to the Gunks (as they are known locally). More than 300 feet of tough conglomerate cap 2,000 feet of Martinsburg

LEFT: *A porcupine balances on a birch branch. Ungainly on the ground, it is a sure-footed climber that feeds on leaves, twigs, and bark.*

RIGHT: *Viewed from Mohonk's Skytop to the northeast, a rocky escarpment known as the Trapps appears to float on a sea of bright autumn foliage.*

shale, a soft sedimentary rock that originated as mud under prehistoric seas. The highest elevations—generally around 2,000 feet, give or take a couple of hundred—are in the northernmost 20 miles.

The Shawangunks present sweeping ridgetop vistas, dramatic cliffs, slopes sprinkled with rocky rubble called talus, valleys crowded with rich forests, exquisite glacial lakes, and several rare ecosystems. The best times to visit are early June, when the countryside all but sinks under the luxuriant bloom of mountain laurel, or early October, when leaf color usually peaks. In this area about 20,000 acres of both public and private land are protected in a primitive, undeveloped state.

Begin with the **Mohonk Preserve❖,** a 6,250-acre privately operated refuge northwest of the college town of New Paltz; the visitor center is on Mountain Rest Road near Route 299. Check out the preserve's Undercliff Carriage Road beside Route 44/55 in the Trapps for a clear picture of geologic underpinnings. On this cut between cliff faces, layers of white and pale gray conglomerate tilt upward at 22-to-45-degree angles. Splashed here and there by red, pink, orange, and black blotches (some mineral-based, some of botanical origin), the tipsy stone layers ripple in and out like undulating battlements on a massive fortress. If the weather is decent, climbers dangle from ropes, slowly scaling the cliffs; the Gunks are the Northeast's number-one rock-climbing site. From late August into November, hundreds of migrating hawks soar along the Trapps.

For a very different perspective, visit the preserve's rock-rift area. In a dimly lit forest, shaded mostly by hemlock and black birch, cushion moss and leaf litter carpet the ground, and numerous narrow gashes break the stony surface. Massive slabs of conglomerate rest here on brittle shale, which has rifted as water seeped through it for thousands

of years. Burdened by gravitation and weakened by fractures, the conglomerate caprock slid over the shale and cracked, opening deep fissures (sometimes called ice caves) 50 to 80 feet deep. During winter, precipitation falls into the crevices and refrigerates the rocks. Ice persists here well into warm weather, when the temperature may be 75 degrees Fahrenheit at the surface, but only in the upper 40s below.

About seven miles southwest on Route 44/55, 12,000 mountainous forested acres that once belonged to a rustic resort are now **Minnewaska State Park Preserve❖.** Just beyond the entrance, a trail through hemlock forest follows a brook rippling over flat stones. The water gathers speed and volume on a downhill course until it becomes Awosting Falls, a wide sheet of water cascading 65 feet into a pool below. Behind the falls, a wall composed of dozens of horizontal layers of rock appears to be painted with muddy red, yellow, and black patterns—as though prehistoric Native Americans had decorated the surface with abstractions. In reality, water has leached minerals from the rocks to create the natural artwork.

ABOVE: *In the Mohonk Preserve, yellow gold-enrod punctuates lavender wild bergamot; both are said to possess healing powers.*
LEFT: *Climbers scale a cliff face in the Near Trapps. Every autumn, these rugged terraces attract numerous migrating hawks.*

An auto road leads to the top of a ridge and the park's namesake lake. Rising almost straight up from the surface of the water, imposing cliffs frame Minnewaska's northern shoreline. Massive blocks and slim sheets of stone suggest polished marble inlaid into a perfectly fitting masonry mosaic. On the east and south, mixed deciduous and conifer forest flows to the shoreline. In early May along the edge of the intensely blue-green pool, shadbushes put out their clouds of tiny white, spidery blossoms.

Minnewaska, which covers 34 acres and measures 78 feet at its deepest point, is one of five sky lakes that glaciers quarried into the ridgetops of the area. When the bottom of the mile-high ice rode over faults, it fused with blocks of stone already split and loosened along fault lines. As the glacier traveled on, it carted away the captured stone, eventually leaving big beachless basins. The clear waters that fill them are naturally acidic and devoid of nutrients. Hardly anything, plant or animal, lives in them; no one has seen a fish in Minnewaska since 1922. A four-mile hiking trail runs from Minnewaska west to **Awosting,** the largest of the

ABOVE: *A blue-winged teal reveals its characteristic pale-blue wing patch; the white marking in front of the duck's eye identifies this individual as a male.*

RIGHT: *North/South Lake, viewed from Sunset Rock, is one of the many waterfowl refuges nestled amid the Catskills.*

sky lakes, which spreads grandly over 90 acres and plummets 90 feet.

Park trails and carriageways also lead to numerous stunning vistas. A barren, rocky promontory called Gertrude's Nose overlooks treetops in wide, deep Palmaghatt Ravine. West of Gertrude's Nose, another trail ascends 2,100 feet above the valley to Castle Point, where on clear days visitors can see into five states. Because the Shawangunk Ridge is in the heart of the Atlantic hawk flyway, these locations are splendid for sighting birds of prey by the dozens on clear, windy autumn days.

Due west of Minnewaska—about five miles southeast of Ellenville off Route 52—**Ice Caves Mountain❖** is both a commercial operation and a national natural landmark. Stop first to admire the view at Sam's Point, a protruding ledge that occupies a bit of open space 2,255 feet above the valley. Five states—New York, New Jersey, Pennsylvania, Connecticut, and Massachusetts—are visible on good days, and sometimes the spires of Manhattan skyscrapers can be spotted.

A short drive leads to the Ice Caves—which are indeed icy but not actually caves. Here fissures have split off colossal conglomerate blocks from a mother megarock to create a series of rockbound alleys. At the finale of the guided tour, two enormous blocks have tilted together to form a natural A-frame.

Follow the road that loops around this property to reach **Lake**

Maratanza, another sky lake, at the top of the mountain. The bedrock plateau surrounding the lake is home to an unusual pygmy forest; this ecosystem, called dwarf pine plains, is the only one of its kind in the world. The trees are pitch pines, a common species here, which normally grow 20 to 35 feet tall. Barely reaching five feet, the pygmies at Maratanza are not genetic curiosities but rather the product of an impoverished environment. The topsoil—so thin as to be almost nonexistent—is low on nutrients and high in acid, and fires bedevil the little trees on a fairly frequent basis.

North of the Shawangunks lies Rip Van Winkle country and an altogether different breed of mountains. Small in stature by western U.S. standards—averaging about 3,500 feet, although two surpass 4,000—but quite picturesque, the hazy, purplish blue **Catskill Mountains** have attracted tourists, statesmen, and artists since early in the nineteenth century. In composition, they differ from the neighboring Shawangunks, even though both are largely sedimentary in origin; the most common materials are horizontally layered greenish sandstone

---

OVERLEAF: *In Catskill Mountain House (1855) Jasper Cropsey showcased a now vanished resort hotel that flourished for a century. Its fine view— a reward for hikers up the Wall of Manitou—remains undiminished.*

LEFT: *The Escarpment Trail threads through the green-hued sandstone outcroppings of the Catskill Mural Front to Sunset Rock's legendary vistas.*
RIGHT: *Widespread throughout the region, the coyote is swift, indefatigable, and adaptable; its omnivorous diet ranges from insects, rodents, and frogs to plants and larger mammals such as deer.*

and reddish shale. Geologically, they are part of the southeastern tip of the Allegheny Plateau. A rocky mass left when a shallow inland sea receded more than 200 million years ago, the Catskills were dissected by streams and further sculpted by glaciers. Some 1,500 miles of small rivers and trout-filled creeks (named kills by Dutch settlers) flow among them, nurturing forests of oak, maple, birch, spruce, fir, and hemlock.

Within **Catskill Park❖** along the mountains' eastern edge facing the Hudson is an enormous scarp that geologists dubbed the **Catskill Mural Front.** A mecca within a grand scenic mecca, the top of the sheer cliff offers a 50-mile Hudson River panorama of mountains, lakes, and forests from Albany south almost to the Hudson Highlands. Natty Bumppo, James Fenimore Cooper's fictional wilderness hero, said that one could see "all creation" from up here. Visitors may hike to the Wall of Manitou (the scarp's more romantic name) via the Escarpment Trail on Mountain House Road (Route 23A) near Haines Falls or drive within 200 yards on South Lake Road off Route 18.

Three miles north of Palenville off Route 23A is **Kaaterskill Falls,** which is often called the jewel of the upper Catskills. In 1993 state geologists remeasured the height of the falls at 230 feet, a slight downgrade from the 260 usually listed. Even though the plunge occurs in two stages, many consider it the state's tallest waterfall. The first drop alone exceeds the plunge at Niagara, albeit with a much, much smaller volume. Here a ribbon of water flings itself over a sandstone ledge to land in a plunge pool atop a second ledge. Wispy strands of water make the second, shorter leap, then reassemble as a creek churning around boulders on a downhill zigzag.

Farther north toward Albany, **the Helderbergs** (meaning bright, or clear, mountains) beckon. Like the Catskills, they are part of the eastern

LEFT: *This nineteenth-century illustration captures the vivid color of the northern pitcher plant, which digests insects in its curved tubular leaves.*
RIGHT: *Although it cannot match Niagara's roaring cataracts, two-tiered Kaaterskill Falls actually ranks as New York State's tallest waterfall.*

limit of the Allegheny Plateau; but the family resemblance is limited, and they never rise above 2,000 feet. The best place to experience them is **John Boyd Thacher State Park❖** on Route 157, 18 miles west of the capital. The sheer cliff called the Helderberg Escarpment runs through here, and from an overlook, the view extends north and east, well past Albany into Adirondack foothills, Vermont's Green Mountains, and the Taconic range along the border of Massachusetts.

The park offers multiple hiking trails and other forms of recreation, but the chief attraction is the **Indian Ladder Trail,** a half-mile walk about a hundred feet below the edge of the scarp. The cliff face curves gently, a composition of hundreds of thin horizontal layers (mostly one to three inches thick) of two types of limestone, suggesting a grimy multitiered pastry. The rocks (named for locations where they were first identified) originated as sediments at the bottom of a shallow inland sea that disappeared about 230 million years ago. The cliff top, or caprock, is Coeymans Limestone, a tough, resistant substance. About 50 feet thick, it looms over the trail like a giant beetling brow because the next 50 feet are Manlius limestone, a much softer material that has eroded more rapidly. Between the two variations on the limestone theme is a thin layer of shale.

Fossil remains of small prehistoric marine animals embedded in the limestone layers make the escarpment one of the richest fossil lodes in the world. Groundwater seeping through the porous rock walls occasionally erupts with force, showering 20 to 30 feet down like miniature waterfalls—but rarely sprinkling hikers.

CENTRAL AND WESTERN NEW YORK:
THE ALLEGHENY PLATEAU AND THE GREAT LAKES LOWLANDS

T he Finger Lakes. Niagara. The Grand Canyon of the East. Watkins Glen. The western two-thirds of New York is up to its touristic eyeballs with scenic delights, which include some of America's most dramatic natural wonders. Sectioned by streams of varying sizes, the hilly landscape is part of the Allegheny Plateau, a geologic province that extends eastward from the plains along Lake Erie almost to Albany. Although the plateau is tilted, the upward slope is so minuscule that only a geologist would notice. The northern and western edges of the region are two Great Lakes, Ontario and Erie, and the lowlands near their shores. To the south is Pennsylvania and more of the plateau.

At one time or another glaciers enveloped much of the northern United States, but nowhere is the impact of the last ice age more apparent than in the western reaches of New York. Drivers on I-90 or Route 20 between Syracuse and Rochester, for example, can't help noting the seemingly endless array of modest "rolling" hills. Although their origin is not obvious, they are actually drumlins, piles of glacial rubble called till that were rounded by massive ice sheets grinding over them. In the centuries since, vegetation clothed them. In fact, this area on the Ontario Plain is one of the world's greatest drumlin fields. Even though many were destroyed or partitioned by settlements,

LEFT: *Near Ithaca, reed canary grass and spent purple loosestrife stalks edge Lake Cayuga. Because the valley was aligned on the glacier's north-south axis, the lake bed is now exceptionally deep (432 feet).*

farms, and highways, more than 10,000 remain. The glacial heritage hereabouts also includes an abundance of potholes, kettle-hole lakes, eskers, kames, and moraines, not to mention those two inland oceans called Great Lakes. The most dramatic glacial footprints appear in the Finger Lakes region just south of the drumlin field.

The tour for the chapter begins at Syracuse and moves south through the Tully Valley and then west to the college town of Ithaca, an excellent base for visiting the Finger Lakes and a galaxy of gorges of unsurpassed beauty. After a swing northwest to Letchworth and the Genesee's "Grand Canyon of the East," it heads into the state's southwestern corner, then north to Niagara, and finally east along the shore of Lake Ontario to its sandy eastern end, just before the confluence of the Saint Lawrence River.

GLACIAL GHOSTS IN THE MIDDLE OF NEW YORK

The **Clark Reservation❖**, an unusual park on Route 173 between Jamesville and Syracuse, is home to a phantom waterfall and a mysterious lake. When glacial ice departed northern New York between 10,000 and 6,000 years ago, tons of meltwater surged over the terrain, largely limestone formed millions of years earlier. At this site, a monumental cascade poured over a limestone horseshoe 1,300 feet across. Laced with boulders and other debris, the watery torrent plummeted 175 feet and in 2,000 years excavated a ten-acre plunge pool 62 feet deep—the lake. Scientists estimate that the creative flood was greater in volume than the one that pours over the American Falls at Niagara today.

Visitors may hike to the top of the crescent precipice where the deluge once flowed, but they must imagine the waterfall. Now quite calm, the soft green pool below is a rare meromictic lake. In most lakes, "turnovers" occur spring and fall when water at the surface and the bottom mix and mingle. In parts of this lake, the waters (a chilly 43 degrees Fahrenheit year-round) never exchange places, and scientists aren't certain why. At least part of the explanation is that hills and thick forest around the lake block the wind, which usually triggers turnover. Only 11 such lakes exist in the United States, along with a few more worldwide.

Two more meromictic lakes (named Round and Green) are in near-

CENTRAL & WESTERN NEW YORK

25 Miles

25 Kilometers

CANADA

ONTARIO

Watertown

Alexander Corners

EL DORADO BEACH PRESERVE

SOUTHWICK BEACH STATE PARK

LAKEVIEW WILDLIFE MANAGEMENT AREA

Port Ontario

DERBY HILL BIRD OBSERVATORY

Utica

Oneida Lake

GREEN LAKES SP

Chittenango

CHITTENANGO FALLS SP

Cazenovia

Jamesville

Apulia Station

LABRADOR HOLLOW STATE NATURE PRESERVE

Syracuse

Auburn

Otisco Lake

CLARK RESERVATION SP

FILLMORE GLEN SP

Ithaca

BUTTERMILK FALLS STATE PARK

Skaneateles Lake

ROBERT H. TREMAN STATE PARK

Owasco Lake

Cayuga Lake

TAUGHANNOCK FALLS SP

Montour Falls

CHIMNEY BLUFFS STATE PARK

Sodus Bay

MONTEZUMA NWR

Seneca Falls

Seneca Lake

Watkins Glen

WATKINS GLEN SP

LAKE ONTARIO

Rochester

MENDON PONDS COUNTY PARK

Canandaigua Lake

Keuka Lake

Genesee River

LETCHWORTH STATE PARK

Portageville

Olean

ROCK CITY

IROQUOIS NATIONAL WILDLIFE REFUGE

Alabama

TONAWANDA WMA

Salamanca

ALLEGANY STATE PARK

NIAGARA RESERVATION STATE PARK

Niagara Falls

Horseshoe Falls

Niagara R

Buffalo

LAKE ERIE

by **Green Lakes State Park❖,** 11 miles east of Syracuse between Routes 5 east and 290 north. They too are plunge-pool basins carved out by glacial streams, but here the water—falling on shale, which is much softer than limestone—scooped out pools nearly 200 feet deep. The lakes' exotic turquoise color, resembling oceanic waters around Caribbean islands, is produced by a combination of factors. Because the lakes are so deep, no light reflects off the bottom. Containing little plant life or organic debris, the water has the clarity of new windowpanes. Calcium carbonate in the water reflects blue-green light back to the surface while canceling the filtering effect of the organic material that is present.

About ten miles southeast, on Route 13 between the towns of Chittenango and Cazenovia, a picturesque cascade gives its name to **Chittenango Falls State Park❖.** In the Iroquois language Chittenango means "where the waters divide and flow north." At the park, a creek of that name slips through a narrow gorge and over the falls, a 167-foot downpour descending leisurely over a staircase of limestone steps. A trail along the western edge of the falls offers fine views of falling water as well as a broad assortment of wildflowers, ferns, and shrubs. (More than 170 vascular plant species have been noted in the park.)

Some 30 miles south of Syracuse, on Route 91 just south of Apulia Station, the **Labrador Hollow State Nature Preserve❖** protects a little-known natural anomaly. Excavated by glaciers, this long, narrow valley—about half a mile wide with steep walls rising several hundred feet—has a unique botanical character. Although the forest is standard northern hardwood, the heavy shade in the narrow north-south cut has fostered a subalpine plant community more typical of high-mountain bogs in the Adirondacks. Labrador tea grows here, for example, as do insectivorous sundews and pitcher plants. The area's centerpiece is Labrador Pond, a shallow 120-acre body of water largely surrounded by wetlands. On the eastern edge of the preserve, Tinkers Falls spills like a thin, watery ribbon over a ledge into a 50-foot-high natural amphitheater. The preserve's undisturbed habitat makes it a popular destination for migrating birds, especially hawks and waterfowl.

RIGHT: *Magenta-colored spikes of purple loosestrife bloom in a boulder-studded pool beneath Chittenango Falls. This invasive nonnative plant is now rampant in wetlands throughout the eastern United States.*

THE FINGER LAKES AND THE GENESEE RIVER VALLEY

This is a land of long, deep, skinny lakes arrayed on a north-south axis; harsh but exotic gashes in the earth's surface; cool, damp forests; and tumbling waters. According to Native American legend, the digit-like lakes were created when God placed a hand on some of the earth's most beautiful countryside—the chosen land of the Iroquois tribes. (Possibly the Deity used both hands, because there are 11 finger lakes—or perhaps the legend refers only to the 5 eastern lakes.) The six nations of the Iroquois Confederacy (Cayuga, Mohawk, Onondaga, Oneida, Seneca, and Tuscarora) named the lakes for tribes within a larger alliance of nations. From east to west, the lakes are now called Otisco, Skaneateles, Owasco, Cayuga, Seneca, Keuka, Canandaigua, Honeoye, Canadice, Hemlock (the only exception to tribal nomenclature), and Conesus.

Geologists take a different view of the Finger Lakes creation. Much of today's northeastern United States was covered by a shallow inland sea for millions upon millions of years. When the sea vanished eons ago, the older rocks remaining there were eroded by streams that carved a landscape patterned with small river valleys where the lakes are today. The sea also left rock. Compressed by the water and its own weight, thousands of layers of sediment became sturdy sandstone, limestone, and siltstone as well as the weaker, more easily splintered and eroded shale.

About two million years ago, an ice age arrived in North America. In a torturously slow process, glaciers a mile thick repeatedly advanced and retreated over what would become central New York. During the glaciers' back-and-forth travels, tongues of ice dug in and deepened the river valleys. When the ice retreated for the last time, only 14,000–12,000 years ago, water melting from the glacier filled the troughs it had created. It also left behind a ridge called a moraine composed of tons of rocky, sandy rubble (glacial till) that dammed the ends of the valleys. The rivers became long, deep, skinny lakes.

The Finger Lakes range in length from 3.5 miles (Canadice) to 38 miles (Cayuga) and in depth from 30 feet (Honeoye) to 634 feet (Seneca). Because the measurement reaches only to glacial deposits, not to rock bottom, the troughs are actually deeper. The lakes' azure blue beauty can be glimpsed only fleetingly from highways and a

ABOVE: *A stone stairway carries the Rim Trail above Buttermilk Falls. Near the trail, the last leaves of a sumac have turned crimson; its fruit remains throughout the winter, sustaining many birds and mammals.*

handful of parks. They are best appreciated from the water, and four boat excursions are available on Seneca, Canandaigua, Cayuga, Skaneateles, and Keuka—the last the oddball of the group with a forked shape resembling a slingshot.

The grinding, gouging glacial bulldozing also produced notched hanging valleys, which began as valleys of tributary streams that flowed into rivers, the ones that turned into lakes. The glacial ice tongues cut the major valleys so deeply that the tributary valleys were left suspended about 600 feet higher than lake surfaces. With no stoppers to plug them the way the moraines plugged the lakes, newly established tributary streams spilled over and rushed through the hanging valleys, sculpting them over thousands of years into deep, stone-walled gorges. The layered walls of shale and the harder rocks eroded at different rates. Where water encountered tough limestone or sandstone, erosion was slower, yielding waterfalls and other cascading currents.

As attractive as the Finger Lakes are, the hanging valleys are the true glory of this region, which boasts the densest concentration of such glens in the United States. Together, glens and lakes constitute one of America's greatest scenic spectacles in a relatively compact area. Most glen parks are not open for visitors until May, because they

51

LEFT: *Surrounded by autumnal maples and ashes, Buttermilk Falls skitters over multilayered rock in its 500-foot descent. Such breathtakingly deep, steep-sided gorges are common in the Finger Lakes region.*
RIGHT: *Never far from water even in winter, a muskrat, its long tail curled forward, perches on an icy lake. Webbed hind feet make these rodents powerful swimmers; their lustrous fur makes them prey for trappers.*

fill with snow and ice during winter, and trails must be cleared. In spring the flow of water, fed by snowmelt, is most impressive; but October—when foliage flames red, yellow, orange, copper, and all their variations—is the primest of times.

For a first taste of the region's "dancing waters," try one of the most accessible glens, **Buttermilk Falls State Park**❖ on Route 13 on the southern boundary of Ithaca. The showcase water begins its 500-foot descent as a creek, ripping through a steep rock-walled passage and taking several plunges of 10 to 20 feet. Widening as it goes, the stream slips in thin bubbling sheets over the charcoal-colored rock incline. Pausing on a plateau as if to catch its breath, the cascade hisses and fizzes as it negotiates a curve, then resumes its downward slide. It works up to a climactic finish over the final 150 feet, sweeping in an ever-so-slight curve over a layered rock face angled about 45 degrees and stretching roughly 50 feet across. Here the watery sheet unravels into countless threads, spinning down the rocky slide and indeed resembling buttermilk spilling over a tilted table.

A very different spectacle occurs about five miles southwest of Ithaca—also on Route 13—at **Robert H. Treman State Park**❖. In Enfield Glen (the park's centerpiece), a creek of the same name launches a leisurely journey with a whisper. The stream meanders through shadowy forest where sprinklings of maples, beeches, and birches highlight scores of dominant hemlocks. Red squirrels cling to the crusty bark, snorting warnings while silent chipmunks scurry amid ferns at ground level. As the path along the creek inches downward, the gorge walls—sky-high

LEFT: *Gold and pale lavender, New England asters, which can reach a height of seven feet, flourish in Taughannock Falls State Park.*
RIGHT: *Fillmore Glen's lower falls create a lacy bridal-veil effect as they tumble headlong through their glacially sculpted chasm.*

stacks of thin, dark shale that give the ravine an architectural aura—rise steadily higher. Ferns, shrubs, even trees find footholds amid the stacks, creating a luxuriant hanging garden. Here and there, little springs pop from between layers and shower down through dense mats of moss.

The descent grows steeper as the path skirts the precipice along the edge of the creek. The water rapidly builds momentum through a series of drops, writhing and frothing more and more until it reaches the devilish climax of **Lucifer Falls.** Where the ravine walls open into a natural amphitheater, the creek crashes down 115 feet over a dozen or more major drops. The combination of giant steps and even more baby steps in between is called a pulpit falls, and in a bumpy ride the liquid shreds into braids spinning over stone domes and blocks. About a third of the way down, the waters part; heavy flows obscure the rocks at both sides while wispy streamlets dampen the center stones. As sun strikes the surface, the water ignites like flashbulbs exploding against the inky walls. Once it reaches bottom, the creek reassumes its whispering character and, brooklike, flows on.

A few blocks from Cayuga Lake in Ithaca, near the corner of Lake and Falls streets, visitors can marvel at **Ithaca Falls❖,** 150 feet tall and almost as wide. A path leads to a deep pool at the cascade's base, where a massive gush of water spills between wooded rock walls. Like many waterfalls in this land of waterfalls, the Ithaca cascade is also a pulpit falls—a series of resistant rock layers that transform a torrential stream into a frothy, multistepped spectacle.

About 30 miles northeast of Ithaca on Route 38, more aquatic theater

draws an audience at **Fillmore Glen State Park❖.** Little sunlight penetrates the bottom of the park's narrow, decidedly deep gorge thick with hemlocks, maples, oaks, beeches, and birches. The trail follows a stream as it repeatedly changes direction and depth, a pattern mirrored in the sounds it makes—from timid trickling to burbling to rumbling and occasionally roaring like a distant cannonade.

The most dramatic waterscape occurs not far from the park entrance and trailhead. At the lower falls, the brook, which launches its run at the other end of the gorge, rockets over a last big precipice. Leaping past the edge, it strikes a huge "nose" of a boulder—with a little imagination, one can see a stone face under the gushing water—and splits. The streams rejoin in a watery swirl below the face, then diverge again to shoot through two long chutes at right angles to the face. In the cliff wall perpendicular to the falls, soft Moscow shale has eroded under Tully limestone into a huge semicircular alcove that creates an echo chamber reverberating the stream's bombast. Still called the Cowshed, this spot is where grazing cattle cooled off each summer before the glen became a park.

At **Taughannock Falls State Park❖,** eight miles north of Ithaca on Route 89, a level trail leads to the falls beside a wide, shallow creek dotted with numerous small cascades. After three-quarters of a mile, visitors emerge into a grotto facing a towering perpendicular cliff sliced in the middle by the falls. The top half of the cliff below the streaming water is hard sandstone, the bottom softer shale. Because the weaker rock has eroded more rapidly, the sandstone has been undermined and broken away in chunks. Over many centuries the combination of water and weather, and weak and strong rocks, has chiseled a V-shaped notch into the cliff. The forces of nature have also etched into the curving rock face designs

ABOVE: *"The bluebird carries the sky on its back,"* *wrote Thoreau. Here it just perches on a twig with a captured insect.*

LEFT: *Sandstone tops Taughannock Falls, the region's tallest straight-drop cascade; darker shale predominates at the cliff's bottom.*

OVERLEAF: *In the shallows of Lake Cayuga, the summer sun highlights lush waterlilies, purple loosestrife, and marsh grasses in the Montezuma refuge.*

LEFT: *In a lightning swoop, a bald eagle seizes a fish. Once nearly extinct, eagles now breed regularly at the Montezuma refuge where they were reintroduced in 1976.*
RIGHT: *Synchronizing their movements even at rest, Canada geese sleep in a shallow pool. Pilots have reported seeing flocks of migrating Canadas cruising comfortably at 8,000 feet.*

reminiscent of a frieze of bas-reliefs in an ancient Babylonian palace.

At the top, an avalanche of water careens through the V, plummeting 215 feet in a dive that exceeds Niagara's: Taughannock Falls is the tallest straight-drop waterfall in the Northeast. With a layered, multiple-stream effect, the water creates intricate patterns, forming and changing shapes as it descends. Blasting into a 30-foot-deep pool at the base of the cliff, hundreds of gallons of water filigree upward into swirls of mist, briefly shrouding the cliff art above.

At its shallow northern end, Cayuga Lake becomes a marsh, site of the **Montezuma National Wildlife Refuge❖**, 7,000 acres of wetlands managed primarily for waterfowl on Routes 20 and 5 five miles east of Seneca Falls. Tens of thousands of birds stop here every year, especially during seasonal migrations. Smack in the middle of one of the busiest lanes on the Atlantic Flyway, the refuge has recorded more than 300 avian species, as well as some 70 "accidentals" that have visited once or twice. The greatest numbers appear in the last half of November, when tens of thousands of birds touch down in the refuge, including 50,000 Canada geese and 25,000 to 50,000 mallard and black ducks. (There is little variety, however, and the weather is foul.)

Mid-October is tops for species density. Visitors following the 3.5-mile self-guided wildlife drive among the pools have an excellent chance of spotting American wigeon, northern pintail, blue-winged teal, redheads, common goldeneyes—or all of the above—paddling about and feeding among dense stands of marsh grasses and cattails. Observation towers provide a panoramic view of the soupy pools and likely sightings of hooded and common mergansers, buffleheads, and

other ducks. A sudden blue flash streaking into the water is bound to be a belted kingfisher that will shoot up in seconds with a small fish clasped in its beak. Shorebirds and wading birds arrive in mid-August and are on hand through mid-October. At least nine members of the sandpiper clan are common, and several others are occasional visitors. The greatest number of shorebirds arrive in September.

Spring is almost as good. Some 12,000–15,000 snow geese land on the pools, raising the noise level appreciably. Part of the refuge is wooded uplands, and in the first two weeks of May at least 15 warbler species are common visitors, and a dozen sparrow species are also likely. Although ospreys rarely venture far from seacoasts and are seldom seen in central New York, from late April through June visitors can observe the whole osprey nesting ritual—from courtship through the fledging of chicks—thanks to nesting platforms erected in front of the visitor center. Now and then an osprey parent circles above the marsh and abruptly zips down feet-first into the water, emerging moments later with a futilely flapping carp in its grasp.

Montezuma was the first site selected by the state's Department of Environmental Conservation to reintroduce bald eagles after the species had all but disappeared from New York because widespread use of the pesticide DDT disrupted the birds' ability to reproduce. The reintroduction program began in 1976, and today nesting bald eagles return to Montezuma each year. Since 1987, they have produced viable young on a regular basis. Youngsters fledge by mid-July, and they and their parents are often visible perching on trees around Tschache (pronounced shockey) Pool.

Almost 40 miles south, the village of Watkins Glen borders the southern end of Seneca Lake. Tour boats depart from here for excursions on Seneca, at 634 feet the deepest of the Finger Lakes and one of the most beautiful. At the other end of the town's main drag (Route 14) is the primary reason for visiting: **Watkins Glen State Park❖.** A sensational blend of water and stone, gravity and motion, the glen is one of America's premier spectacles, king of gorges in a landscape of dazzling water displays. The water passage along 1.5 miles of gorge trail is very narrow and deep.

Glimpsed first at its upper end, Glen Creek is a quick but quiet stream. In short order water is churning wildly downward, slipping through rocky passageways, diving over ledges, rippling along gorge walls in a series of sensuous curves, and whirling in circular basins called plunge pools. Although the stones' graceful contours suggest the inspired craftsmanship of a sculptor of genius, they represent centuries of scouring and polishing by sand and gravel. Some are so smooth that they appear abraded and burnished; others are edged and inscribed like sophisticated pottery. The gorge walls tower 100 to 300 feet above the water, and even on the sunniest days parts of the trail are almost in darkness. Nurtured by deep shadows and water seeping through layers of rock, a gardeny mat of moss and ferns cloaks the walls.

Near the halfway point, a gossamer veil of sun-tinted water sprays from the walls above, and the trail travels behind it. Here at Rainbow Falls, weak shale at the bottom of the cliff has weathered away to a ledge running behind the falls, creating a unique and exciting viewpoint for visitors. Below the trail, a much denser, stormier stream careens over multiple cascades in the chasm's main channel until the

---

RIGHT: *At dawn, a willow tree is silhouetted against the blue expanse of Seneca Lake. In addition to trout, perch, and pike, saltwater fish have been caught here, fueling theories of a subterranean sea passage.*

falls and the main stream meet in one of those curvy pools.

Beyond lies a long progression of pools where water swirls and spills gracefully from one to the next in a fountainlike display worthy of a great botanical garden. Then the walls open wider, arcing in a great curve called the Cathedral. At the apex, a crystal rope called Central Cascade vaults 65 feet downward, the tallest waterfall in the glen. With increasing vigor, the water charges through slender chutes it helped to carve, often flinging itself recklessly into space at the end of a ledge, airborne until it bashes and bounces over boulders on the next level. Such is Cavern Cascade, where the trail once again slips behind falls, a passionate torrent that plunges and dissolves over a stone dome about 60 feet below. Swirling around a pool, the water works itself into a whipped-cream froth, then regains direction and rushes to the next frantic dive, Minnehaha Falls, a shorter, zigzagging drop. After its wild ride, the creek finds its way quietly and conventionally out of the park.

Shequaga Falls❖ at the end of Main Street in Montour Falls, two miles south of Watkins Glen on Route 14, is a broad, fairly straightforward cascade. Appearing from under a bridge at its highest point, the water drops calmly, almost in slow motion, in its descending journey of 165 feet. Following a gentle S curve coming across the top, it eases over several tiers and finally glides down a long slope and a handful of small stairs to a wide pool.

More falling water beckons on the northwestern edge of the Finger Lakes region. Flowing north from Pennsylvania to Lake Ontario, the **Genesee River** becomes part of a spectacular exhibition as it enters the glacially excavated gorge at the heart of 17-mile-long **Letchworth State Park❖,** on Routes 436 and 390. Near the park's southern tip at Portageville, the river plummets through a sequence of dramatic waterfalls undramatically named Upper, Middle, and Lower.

A horseshoe-shaped Niagaralike cataract, Upper Falls handles a whopping volume of water that plunges 70 feet. Agitated into whitewater rapids, the river bounces along banks lined with broad stepped shelves of rock that suggest a theatrical stage. Middle Falls is the biggest,

---

LEFT: *At Cavern Cascade, a carefully constructed trail snakes through the great gorge at Watkins Glen. Deep and narrow, the gorge is an exquisite combination of rock formations and swirling, tumbling water.*

reaching a width of 285 feet in a perpendicular plunge of 107 feet. The torrential flow of these two falls is so dense it completely obscures the erosion-resistant sandstone superstructure that gives Upper and Middle falls their shapes and patterns. At Lower Falls—a shorter, multispill cascade more like those in the nearby Finger Lakes glens—the river bursts through a narrow gash in the gorge 75 feet deep. Because the rock here is soft shale, erosion has altered the look of Lower Falls many times.

For a splendid view of Upper and Middle falls, follow the road to Inspiration Point atop cliffs rising hundreds of feet above the river. A mountain of mist spawned by the cascades spirals upward, and on sunny days the rays transform the spray into shimmering rainbows. The Seneca, who called this spot Seh-Ga-Hun-Da (Vale of Three Falls), believed Middle Falls was so beautiful that the sun was compelled to pause at midday and admire the scene. In 1839, before a railroad trestle spanned the air above Upper Falls, Hudson River School artist Thomas Cole captured the two falls on canvas. This painting, entitled *Portage Falls on the Genesee,* now hangs in the Seward House Museum in Auburn, New York, about 25 miles southwest of Syracuse.

Farther along Park Road, the main thoroughfare through Letchworth's more than 14,300 acres, another viewpoint overlooks the Big Bend of the Genesee and the cleft proclaimed the Grand Canyon of the East. Because it measures only about 550 feet at its deepest, it cannot be favorably compared statistically with the Grand Canyon of Arizona, which is ten times deeper. This eastern canyon does not lack for beauty, however. Slopes too steep to be logged decades ago still support 300- to 400-year-old hemlocks with trunks three to four feet in diameter and 500- to 600-year-old Eastern redcedars.

In the seven square miles of Letchworth's southern end, 25 warbler species have nested, more than in any other single site in the world. All told, 36 warbler species pause in the park from April through June. May brings peak migration numbers; June is tops for nesting and the arrival of chicks.

RIGHT: *Commissioned by friends of Governor William Seward, Thomas Cole's* **Portage Falls on the Genesee** *(1839) depicts the Upper and Middle Falls.*

OVERLEAF: *On seeing Niagara Falls, historian Thomas Macauley wrote: "A man who has never looked on Niagara has but a faint idea of a cataract."*

NIAGARA AND THE
ERIE-ONTARIO LOWLANDS

In New York's southwestern corner, about six miles south of Olean on Route 16, visitors can walk the "streets" of **Rock City❖**. This commercial attraction offers an impressive assembly of megaboulders, many as tall as eight-story buildings and equally thick. Formed about 325 million years ago, the quartz conglomerate rock foundation is a hard sedimentary stone made of milky white quartz pebbles embedded in a slurry of sand and gravel that hardened into a natural cement. Also known as pudding stone, this type of rock originally protruded from hillsides in colossal beds. When fragile shale beneath the beds eroded, leaving the conglomerate without support, massive blocks snapped free. They moved downhill, inch by inch, over thousands of years via a process known as soil creep.

The great bubbly blobs wound up leaning against one another in a loose grid of alleys, lanes, tunnels, and quasi-caves resembling a city. Up close, with their lumpen forms and multitude of wrinkles and crinkles, the stones suggest enormous, very doughy pastries studded with white nuts, frosted with mantles of moss, and festooned with ferns of various persuasions. Isolated goliaths assume a variety of shapes—from a pointed top like a pyramid or Native American tepee to monstrous slabs reminiscent of monuments in a public square.

About 20 miles west at Salamanca on Route 17, **Allegany State Park❖** occupies nearly 95 square miles, New York's largest outside Adirondack Park. Although the region was heavily logged in the nineteenth century, the hilly landscape is now covered by tall second-growth, self-propagated hardwoods—beeches, sugar and red maples, yellow and black birches, oaks, hickories, white ashes, and more—some nearing the century mark. On about October 10 they burst into a brilliant, colorful display.

The dense stands of tall trees, and diverse habitats among them, attract numerous nesting birds and other wildlife. A dozen raptor species—including bald eagles—are regulars. Five kinds of woodpeckers are also fond of this park, along with warblers galore—22 species nest here. Riots of wildflowers line the roadsides during spring. At the Thunder Rocks Overlook, massive conglomerate rocks like those that created Rock City huddle on a hilltop, dwarfing human visitors.

In western New York, to head north along Lake Erie toward the source of the Niagara River is all but obligatory. Although it isn't one of the world's great rivers like the Nile or the Mississippi, at only 37 miles long the Niagara puts on one hell of a show. Technically a strait running along the Canadian border between Lakes Erie and Ontario, the Niagara River is charged by water from four great lakes: Erie, Superior, Huron, and Michigan, an outpouring of 202,000 cubic feet of water per second.

After glaciers receded about 14,000–12,000 years ago, meltwater filled the upper Great Lakes and sought outlets to the sea. The main discharge from Erie became the present-day river—other routes dried up because today's course is the lowest—and began cutting the Niagara Gorge. In the more than 12,000 years since, the waterway eroded upstream about seven miles. About A.D. 1300 the river split, creating twin cataracts, and **Niagara Falls** joined the ranks of major-league American natural wonders along with Yellowstone, Yosemite, and the Grand Canyon. The falls are even more awesome considering that 50 to 75 percent of the river's natural flow is siphoned off to generate electrical power and to fill a canal before the stream arrives at the precipices.

Indians named the spectacle Niagara, or "the bottleneck," because the falls and rapids made it impossible to travel from one lake to another. Louis Hennepin, a Belgian who became a priest and was chaplain to the French explorer La Salle, became one of the first Europeans to see the falls when the Seneca led him there in 1678. After one look, Father Hennepin dropped to his knees, exclaiming, "The universe does not afford its parallel!" The overwhelmed cleric estimated the height of the falls at 600 feet; in fact, they are less than 200, but awe-inspiring nevertheless.

A great way to appreciate the phenomenon of the falls is to track them from their origin at the eastern end of Goat Island via a short bridge-crossing from the city of Niagara Falls. As it curves around Buffalo, the river is a wide fast-flowing stream. The island then splits it into two channels, initially mild white-water streams. The Upper Cascades, which preview the big show, are best observed from Three Sister Islands, reached by footbridges on the south side of Goat Island. The Canadian channel, which carries 90 percent of the river's flow, becomes the Canadian, or Horseshoe, Falls.

The waters then forsake peace, rushing around boulders and over short slopes of rock, a couple of feet at first, then drops of six, ten, or

more feet. Seeming to swallow themselves, waves dip down deep into gullies, then burst upward in bubbly white giddiness. As they grow bigger, the waves lunge forward insanely, and the water pools into fleeting mosaics of turquoise, teal, jade, black, gray, and white. The sound also mounts in intensity—as though a battery of howitzers on the edge of the gorge were firing at some alien presence.

Terrapin Point, the western tip of Goat Island, overlooks **Horseshoe Falls,** a 2,500-foot notch in the precipice over which the river plunges 167 feet. From the unseen water surface below, a colossal column of mist soars upward like smoke belched by a chimney, occasionally obscuring the view and drenching onlookers.

For a clear look at **American Falls,** head for Prospect Point in **Niagara Reservation State Park❖** (oldest state park in the United States), a few blocks away. Taller than its Canadian neighbor at 176 feet, this cascade spills over a rim 1,100 feet across. At both falls, the water pitches over a hard, erosion-resistant surface, a type of limestone called Lockport dolostone that is 72 feet thick. Beneath it, a 61-foot layer of Rochester shale erodes easily, crumbling and leaving the dolostone without support so that periodically part of it collapses from its own weight. Tons of talus, or rock rubble, lie at the bottom of American Falls, turning the water into a sea of suds when it hits. With its much greater volume of water, Horseshoe Falls has swept such debris away and hollowed a plunge pool 190 feet deep in the riverbed.

Approaching the edge of American Falls, the river is an emerald liquid. Once over, it separates into pale jade streamers alternating with white ribbons. At the point closest to the path, water billows, shoots out and up, and then drops as though a fountain were set in the stone directing movement and pattern—an explosion of water. From here, visitors can see a third cascade where a rocky island divides a slender strip from the main American flow—**Bridal Veil Falls.** Along the length of the American panorama a curtain of mist floats upward from the tumble of boulders at the base. At Prospect Point visitors may board the *Maid of the Mist,* a tour boat that is essential to experiencing

LEFT: *Viewed from a sheer cliff face in Whirlpool State Park, the Niagara churns furiously from the falls toward Lake Ontario. The river is unnavigable until it reaches Lewiston, seven miles from its terminus.*

the falls. The boat chugs toward the heart of the falling water, past American Falls to the base of the Canadian—safe and sane but close enough to feel the might and majesty of Niagara.

The river continues barreling downstream in varying degrees of white water. At **Whirlpool State Park❖** it rounds a bend between towering cliffs and whips itself into a full-fledged frenzy again, forming a frothy white V in the green current. The notch shreds and spins into a shifting series of powerful eddies that spiral about at a dizzying rate—a whirlpool, more than 100 feet deep, that is no place for a canoeist. Once past the swirling pool, the river makes a sharp right turn between gorge walls and proceeds toward its rendezvous with Lake Ontario. Although many waterfalls are taller and some boast greater breadth and water volume, Niagara remains the standard by which all others are judged.

Some 35 miles east of Niagara's splendor, near the village of Alabama on Route 77, departing glaciers left an enormous lake about 10,000 years ago. After thousands of years, much of it had become swampland. In 1958 the federal government turned nearly 11,000 acres into the **Iroquois National Wildlife Refuge❖.** The state added contiguous lands: **Tonawanda Wildlife Management Area❖** on the western boundary, **Oak Orchard Wildlife Management Area❖** on the east. All told, about 20,000 acres are now set aside for wildlife, not only wooded swamps but wet and dry meadows, marshes, upland forests, dense thickets of shrubs and vines, and cropland cultivated for the animals.

At numerous overlooks beside ponds, pools, and marshes, visitors can park and peer through binoculars at the wild residents. At Cayuga Overlook on the edge of Tonawanda WMA, large ponds stretch to dense woodlands. The woods harbor a rookery with 200–300 great blue heron nests, and by June some 700 herons are in residence. The big blue-gray birds are seen all over the refuge, frozen in position like rigid sentinels, stalking the waters in slow motion to snatch unwary fish, or launching forth with slow, graceful pumps of their powerful wings.

On the refuge's eastern side, the Onondaga Trail passes an open swamp studded with dead trees and stumps among thick stands of cattails and grasses. The muskrat are visible only at dawn or dusk, but for most of the day red-winged blackbirds buzz and bounce from the reeds, ducks and geese drift across the murky water, and painted turtles line up to sunbathe on fallen logs. The trail enters a marshy woodland, a good place to find warblers (including nesting prothonotary warblers), scarlet tanagers, wood thrushes, vireos, and other songbirds. Some 25 warbler species stop at Iroquois each year, and a few more are "irregulars." May 10–21 is the best time to see warblers.

In the spring, populations peak for all species: 266 have been noted at Iroquois. Waterfowl produce the biggest numbers. In a good year, 65,000 Canada geese pause during migration. An average year yields 40,000, and their numbers have reached 88,000. In addition, 24 duck species appear. The population of all waterfowl in a normal spring is 80,000.

In the midst of the drumlin district below Lake Ontario, **Mendon Ponds County Park** (six miles southeast of Rochester on Route 65) is like a glacial theme park. Rivers running at tremendous pressure below glaciers shaped sand and gravel into long winding ridges called eskers, and when the ice melted, sediment that had accumulated in depressions in the ice was deposited in conical hills known as kames. Slow-melting ice produced kettle holes, some of which filled with water and became ponds.

On the lakeshore about 35 miles east of Rochester is one of the most exotically beautiful preserves in the eastern United States, **Chimney Bluffs State Park**. Head east on the road marked "Seaway Trail" (Route 104A) about two miles east of Sodus Bay to Lake Bluff Road. Turn north and follow signs to the Lake Bluff Campground, continuing on a zigzag course about six miles past the campground to the lake. A winding path that overlooks the lake is accessible from a trail about 100 yards from the parking lot.

A short walk brings into view the object of the quest: the bluffs. These lakeside bulwarks have eroded into an assembly of mystical formations: pyramidlike pinnacles; slender slabs—some with big notches gouged into them; twisted, steeplelike spires; roller-coasterish dips and rises; ramparts and towers with jagged edges; elongated buttresses stretching down toward the water. Virtually naked to the sky (only tiny patches of wispy vegetation cling to them), the earthworks shade from a flat yellow to dusty red—the look of old adobe—contrasting sharply with the blue and green patchwork of the lake licking the shore below.

A large colony of bank swallows buzz around the accidental architecture. The plain little gray-and-white speedsters swirl up from nesting burrows tunneled into the cliffs. In total, the scene suggests the ruins of

an ancient Sumerian fortress abandoned centuries ago. The fortress is in reality a giant drumlin, one of a series of glacial relics along the lake. Composed of sand, gravel, mud, and other debris rounded into a hill by ice, the drumlin was battered and shaped for thousands of years by wind, waves, and wicked weather of all sorts. The bluffs are rich in a gummy clay that has held them together like cement despite the conspiracy of the elements.

At the southeastern corner of Lake Ontario, on Sage Creek Drive off Route 104B, a 50-acre preserve perches on a perpendicular bluff high above the water. **Derby Hill Bird Observatory**❖ is the number-one spot in the Northeast for watching hawks during spring migration. Each year 15 species sail past, often in heavy concentrations. In the fall, the cast changes as gulls, terns, and waterfowl fly by the promontory.

Along the sparsely populated eastern end of Lake Ontario, long stretches of beach still swell with tall, elegantly mounded sand dunes—muffins from the oven of an eccentric baker. Although such complexes have been destroyed across most of the Great Lakes, at **Lakeview Wildlife Management Area**❖ on Route 3 (10.5 miles north of Port Ontario), nearly four miles of barrier beach front Lake Ontario—the longest undisturbed complex of this type on the lake. Some dunes reach 60 feet in height, rivaling the Indiana Dunes on Lake Michigan. The beach and the woodland behind it are loaded with warblers during spring migration, and fall migrators include large numbers of hawks, shorebirds, and waterfowl.

The barrier dunes protect a wetland complex between the beach and the highway—a 2,400-acre marsh basin encompassing five ponds and four streams. Visitors should explore it by boat if possible. An observation tower affords wide-angle views of the marsh and its inhabitants. Nesting waterbirds include American and least bitterns (usually hiding in cattails), black terns, and a variety of ducks.

Also on Route 3 and adjacent to Lakeview, **Southwick Beach State Park**❖ contains the only freshwater dune system in the state park system. A nature trail leads to a protective boardwalk crossing the delicate

---

LEFT: *In Chimney Bluffs State Park, an eerie moonscape overlooks the placid expanse of Lake Ontario. Wind and water created the stark contours of this fantastical shoreline, which is actually a glacial drumlin.*

ABOVE: *Ornithologists believe many waterfowl, such as these snow geese, migrate in family groups, allowing young birds to learn the best routes.*

dunes along Lake Ontario. The area is like a sandy garden of plants that can tolerate the brutal conditions of a dunescape: American beach grass, artemisia, cottonwood trees, and a rare shrub, the dune willow.

Remote but worthwhile, **El Dorado Beach Preserve❖** is off Route 3 where it intersects Stony Creek Road near Alexander Corners. Follow Stony Creek Road west 1.3 miles to an unmarked dirt road (Grandjean Road). Where it forks, stay left and go almost a mile to a gateway. Enter and keep bearing left on a grassy track .2 miles to a parking area and a sign reading "El Dorado Shores."

On this 360-acre refuge, a pair of rocky peninsulas, pockmarked with small plant-and-bug–filled pools, project into Lake Ontario. The preserve attracts a significant and diverse concentration of fall-migrant shorebirds: spotted, white-rumped, least, semipalmated, and western sandpipers; various plover, including black-bellied and killdeers; ruddy turnstones; greater and lesser yellowlegs; common snipes, godwits, dowitchers, and many more. The birds pause here from July through September, their arrival and departure times depending on the species. The greatest variety and numbers occur the last week of August and first week of September. From August through early October, the redcedar forest behind the beach throbs with hyperactive migratory songbirds. In addition, the southern edge of the preserve also contains one of the few relatively undisturbed high-sand-dune communities remaining along Lake Ontario.

RIGHT: *On Ontario's southern shore, sunset gilds a rocky pool in El Dorado Beach Preserve, a stopover for migrating songbirds and waterfowl.*

THE NORTH COUNTRY:

ADIRONDACK PARK AND THE
SAINT LAWRENCE AND
CHAMPLAIN VALLEYS

Remote and thinly populated by humanity, New York's North Country is the wildest place in the Mid-Atlantic region. The rugged tree-shrouded mountains and foothills that dominate the landscape here, known as the Adirondacks, occupy the northeastern corner of New York, accounting for about a quarter of the state's area. The range is not even remotely related to the Allegheny Plateau, which is the foundation for most of the rest of New York, nor is it kin to the Appalachians on the east, or the Berkshires, or the White or Green mountains.

Actually an oval-shaped dome sprawling over 11,000 square miles, the Adirondacks are anchored with rock roots that extend as deep as nine miles into the earth. Although geologists have yet to understand completely the complex process that created the Adirondack dome, the range originated as ocean-bottom sedimentary layers that, under intense heat and pressure below ground, metamorphosed into a hodgepodge of different rocks. Although these rocks are now about 1.1 billion years old—some of the oldest on earth—the foundations of the mountains that enclose them are comparatively youthful, only some 10 million years old. Once the substance and fundamental shape of the mountains were established, glaciers spent more than a million years redecorating the landscape with ravines, lakes, ponds, wetlands, and other features.

LEFT: *In the Adirondacks, evergreens and deciduous trees dressed for autumn brighten the landscape around Eagle Lake. The Adirondacks' current mix of conifers and hardwoods dates back about 2,000 years.*

The name Adirondack appeared later, born of war between the Iroquois and their bitter enemies, the Algonquin. According to legend, the Iroquois scornfully called their adversaries "Ratirontacks," meaning "those who eat bark." The insult characterizes the Algonquin as inept hunters forced to eat tree bark to avoid starvation. European settlers made few forays into the area until after 1850. Unbridled exploitation of nature's resources followed, and in its wake wholesale environmental destruction: clear cutting of vast forests, open pit and strip mines, water pollution, erosion, wildfires, destruction of fisheries, and overhunting of wildlife.

Spurred by the general public, which had discovered the delights of Adirondack vacations, the state legislature created a regional forest preserve in 1885 and Adirondack Park in 1892. In a direct blow to lumbering interests, the 1894 constitutional convention went further, amending the state constitution with the landmark "forever wild" clause. Land in the state forest preserve must remain in a wild state, never to be leased, sold, or logged. The timber cannot be removed or destroyed by any means—not one tree, ever! Because much land within park boundaries had been sold before the legislators acted, today the park is a public-private patchwork more than 50 percent privately owned. Within the park more than a hundred small towns and villages are inhabited by 130,000 people.

Adirondack Park now encompasses more than six million acres, making it the largest American park of any kind outside Alaska. Yellowstone, Glacier, Olympic, Yosemite, Grand Canyon, and Great Smoky Mountains national parks could all fit inside the Adirondack borders, as could neighboring Vermont. The heart of the park is its namesake mountains, 2,500 of which top 2,000 feet. In the High Peaks area of the east-central part of the park, 42 exceed 4,000 feet, and two of those rise above 5,000. Mount Marcy, at 5,344 feet, is the tallest (it is the highest peak in the state as well). Those with summits above the timberline revel in alpine meadows and tundralike terrain; tiny wildflowers; thick clumps of tough golden grass fluttering in a perpetual breeze; green, gray, red, and golden boulders speckled by lichens;

OVERLEAF: *The view south from Whiteface Mountain, more than 4,800 feet above sea level, reveals the last light of a summer's day illuminating the rumpled, tree-covered peaks and blue alpine lakes of the Adirondacks.*

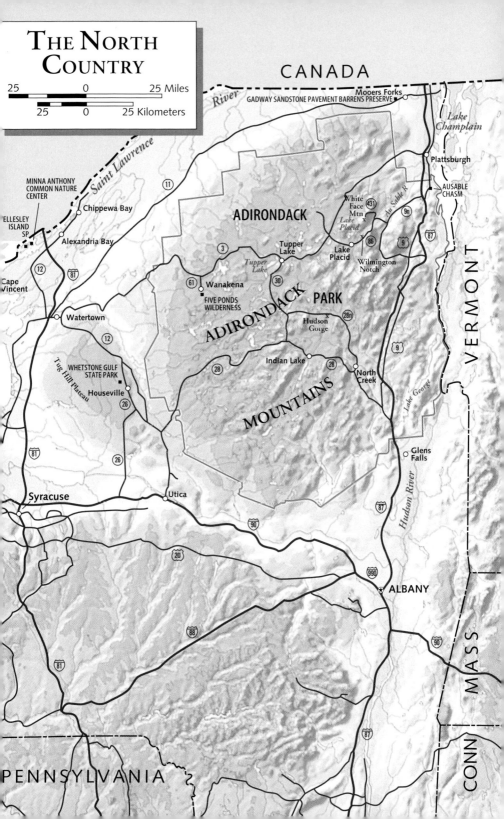

THE NORTH COUNTRY

25   0   25 Miles

25   0   25 Kilometers

CANADA

River

GADWAY SANDSTONE PAVEMENT BARRENS PRESERVE

Mooers Forks

Lake Champlain

Saint Lawrence

Plattsburgh

AUSABLE CHASM

MINNA ANTHONY COMMON NATURE CENTER

Chippewa Bay

ADIRONDACK

White Face Mtn

431

Au Sable R.

9n

ELLESLEY ISLAND SP

Alexandria Bay

11

Lake Placid

86

9

87

Tupper Lake

Lake Placid

Wilmington Notch

3

Cape Vincent

12

81

61 Wanakena

Tupper Lake

30

ADIRONDACK

PARK

VERMONT

FIVE PONDS WILDERNESS

Hudson Gorge

28n

Watertown

12

ADIRONDACK

9

WHETSTONE GULF STATE PARK

28

Indian Lake

28

North Creek

Lake George

Tug Hill Plateau

Houseville

26

MOUNTAINS

81

26

Glens Falls

87

Syracuse

Utica

Hudson River

90

ALBANY

20

990

88

87

81

90

MASS

PENNSYLVANIA

VERMONT

CONN

ABOVE: *In Winslow Homer's watercolor* Mink Pond (1891), *a white water lily, a sunfish, and a frog share an aquatic world in the Adirondacks.*

part-time ponds produced by rain or snowmelt; and above all, glorious vistas of rippling peaks and endless forest.

The forest that blankets 87 percent of the park is a northern latitude blend of red spruce, balsam fir, red and white pine, hemlock, red and sugar maple, yellow birch, black cherry, and more. Of the approximately 2.5 million acres protected as "forever wild," much is second growth—50–100 years old and respectably tall. One-sixth of the park—more than a million acres—is designated wilderness, and 100,000 acres of that is old-growth, virgin forest distinguished by giant trees—such as hemlocks with a girth of 12 feet. Adirondack Park contains the only bona fide wilderness east of the Mississippi River and north of the Everglades.

Sparkling amid the greenery are 2,769 lakes and ponds, 1,345 of them significant enough to be named. More than 50 large lakes and reservoirs have at least one square mile of water surface; Lake Champlain, on the park's eastern border, is the largest body of fresh water in the United States after the Great Lakes. Some 1,200 miles of rivers and

RIGHT: *Purple-flowered pickerelweed thrives in the gentle current of the Oswegatchie River. Both deer and humans find this herb very tasty.*

nearly 31,000 miles of brooks and other small streams wind under the region's overarching tree canopy. Many streams become white-water rapids and waterfalls that rush through rockbound ravines. Roughly 900,000 acres, about 15 percent of the park, is wetlands: swamps, marshes, and bogs that contain a botanical gold mine of hundreds of plant species, many quite rare.

The Adirondacks are the one place in the Mid-Atlantic region where wildlife is almost what it was 300 years ago. Although several species such as wolves and cougars were extirpated by excessive hunting, others are on the comeback trail. Moose returned from Canada and Vermont, and in the 1990s the state began reintroducing lynx—stocky feline predators with tufted ears—whose survival rate in the High Peaks is encouraging. Beavers have also reappeared and are often visible just after sunrise around misty ponds and streams. Mink again caper along creek banks; otters play in lakes and large rivers, although they are not everyday sightings. Fishers, pine marten, porcupines, and bobcat live in the forests, but they all tend to be secretive. Black bears and coyotes appear near campsites, and the bears are also partial to town garbage dumps.

The signature bird of the Adirondacks is the common loon, a magical waterbird with a checkerboard back and a daggerlike beak. Echoing across lakes mornings and evenings, its haunting, yodeling call suggests a hysterical maniac in the neighborhood. The state successfully reintroduced bald eagles and peregrine falcons after they were decimated by DDT. Ravens, giants of the crow family, have rebounded from a popu-

LEFT: *In the northern forest, hunter and hunted are exemplified by the swift, silent lynx (far left), and its prey, the elusive snowshoe hare (near left), which relies on its natural camouflage. In spring, the winter-white hare turns an inconspicuous brown.*

RIGHT: *Black bears thrive in the Adirondack wilderness. Because hibernating bears metabolize uric acid into bone-building calcium, they emerge each spring with undiminished strength.*

lation decline and now croak hoarsely in woodlands and along streams. In most any forested area, ruffed grouse are found—or more likely heard—especially in spring, when the male fans his tail and drums his wings as if imitating a machine gun. Spruce grouse frequent boggy forests containing dense stands of conifers. During spring courtship the black-breasted male with bright red, eyebrow-like combs struts about and beats his wings passionately. The creatures no one wants to meet are the blackflies, bloodthirsty little beasts from hell that can drive a camper over the edge of sanity. The park's wildest areas, especially wetlands, are best avoided during May and June when the blackfly population erupts.

Despite all the protective legislation, the park is almost constantly under siege. Logging and mining continue, although carefully regulated. Acid rain plagues park health, recently transforming 300 clear alpine lakes and ponds into lifeless pools. Real-estate development proceeds apace and is probably the largest single threat to the Adirondacks today. The Northway (I-87), which cleaves the region from Albany to the Canadian border, robbed the area of its isolation, made the

ABOVE: *Below the Thousand Islands Bridge, which links New York and Canada, the Saint Lawrence River is dotted with wooded islands and pleasure boats; beyond, the American Narrows point to Lake Ontario.*

park more accessible, and triggered an exponential increase in seasonal residents. Fortunately organizations such as the Nature Conservancy have preserved thousands of acres of rare and beautiful ecosystems, and the Adirondack Council concentrates on public education while battling developers in the courts and the legislature.

The numerous ways to explore Adirondack Park begin with 1,100 miles of billboard-free highways. Hundreds of miles of trails wind through forests where visitors can take a day hike or camp out for a week or more. Many trails ascend mountains too. Mount Marcy is a long, arduous trek, even for experienced hikers, but Goodnow Mountain, on Route 28N, is a three-mile round trip affording good views of the High Peaks. Mount Jo, southwest of Lake Placid, is just under 3,000 feet and overlooks Heart Lake, with High Peaks stretching before the smaller mountain. Canoe trips are a marvelous way to experience Adirondack wilderness and wildlife. Among many possibilities, the best (in the opinion of some experts) is the route that follows the Fulton Chain of Lakes and the Raquette River from Old Forge to Saranac Lake, nearly 100 miles that can be covered in eight to ten days of canoeing, portaging, and camping. The trip can be made in smaller chunks as well. Many old hands insist that the Adirondacks are best appreciated from above because only when flying in a small plane can one see the full panorama of mountain, lake, and forest, and the immensity of the park. Tour planes are available in the villages of Inlet and Long Lake.

Wise travelers stop at the Visitor Interpretive Centers at Newcomb and Paul Smiths, where exhibits enhance an understanding of the park's natural history and conservation and help visitors plan activities. At the Adirondack Museum in the village of Blue Mountain Lake, 22 rustic buildings plus outdoor exhibits treat regional history, culture, and the natural environment in depth. Except for winter sports enthusiasts and hunters, the Adirondacks have a brief visiting season. The best time is the last two weeks of September, when leaf colors peak. After beginning at the Thousand Islands in the Saint Lawrence River, our tour enters Adirondack Park on the west. The itinerary loops clockwise, first north toward Canada, then east and south along the Vermont border and through the High Peaks, and eventually west, exiting where it entered.

THE SAINT LAWRENCE AND THE ADIRONDACK FOOTHILLS

At the eastern end of Lake Ontario, the Saint Lawrence River begins its crawl toward the Atlantic Ocean. In the roughly 50 miles between the towns of Cape Vincent and Chippewa Bay, the **Thousand Islands**❖— one of North America's most popular vacation destinations—rise above the river's surface. According to a survey conducted by the National Geographic Society, there are 1,793 islands in this stretch (based on qualifying rules—a minimum of one square foot of land, some vegetation cover, and a location above water all year). In the 1930s a treaty divvied up the islands: Canada received the largest number, the United States got the largest in size (with a couple of exceptions), and each country now owns about equal acreage. Another product of the treaty is the international border, which now zigs and zags between islands.

The islands are remnants of a rock bridge (called the Frontenac Arch) linking the Adirondack Mountains with an enormous mass of billion-year-old stone called the Canadian Shield. Glacial ice scoured and sculpted the forms we see today. Although the isles vary con-

LEFT: *The male hairy woodpecker sports a bright red head patch. Because it feasts on bark-boring insects, the bird unwittingly safeguards many trees.* RIGHT: *On Wellesley Island along the Saint Lawrence, tawny grasses sprout near the Eel Bay Trail on the Minna Anthony Common Nature Center preserve.*

siderably in surface area, none is very far above water. They resemble a polyglot flotilla of dark-gray granite vessels ranging from battleships to rowboats, decked out with lush greenery and permanently moored in the Saint Lawrence. Some flash like fire when the sun strikes splotches of bright red granite that explodes from the gray. About 80 percent of the islands have man-made structures on them, mostly summer "cottages." They are best explored by tour boats from Alexandria Bay, the area's touristic capital.

For the most natural slant on river and islands, take Exit 51 off I-81 to **Wellesley Island State Park✦** and the **Minna Anthony Common Nature Center✦,** which occupies 600 of the island's more than 2,400 acres. In addition to an interpretative museum, eight miles of trails investigate such habitats as wooded wetlands, meadows, a beaver swamp, and pitch pine forest growing on granite outcrops. During summer, visitors can take two-hour canoe trips to learn more about the region's ecology and get an up-close perspective on many of the islands.

Southeast of the islands, visitors enter the vast, largely untamed expanses of **Adirondack Park✦** via Route 3. Go south on the road toward Wanakena (about 4.5 miles east of Benson Mines) until it ends to explore one of the park's wilderness areas. Its 95,525 acres make the **Five Ponds Wilderness✦** the largest chunk of virgin forest in the park. Take the trail to Pine Ridge over a series of meandering, glacially formed sand-and-gravel piles called eskers that have been cloaked with old-growth white pine, hemlock, and red spruce. Most of the trees are 250–300 years old. Rising to heights of more than a hundred feet, the trees are shadowy forms amid occasional shafts of dusty light filtering through the canopy.

Wildlife is abundant here, but many creatures become active only around twilight. Browsing where there is enough light for understory plants to grow, small groups of white-tailed deer eye hikers suspiciously. Birds are more likely to be heard than seen because they for-

LEFT: *The fragrant yellow lady's slipper, a native orchid, grows in eastern bogs and moist woodlands.*
RIGHT: *Cutting through layers of ancient limestone, the Au Sable River races toward Lake Champlain.*

age high up in the dense branches. Broad-winged hawks hang out on lower branches, and occasionally one rockets from its perch to pursue a mouse scampering across the forest floor. Hairy woodpeckers may be heard drumming on lifeless trees and sometimes seen. A curious gray jay may drop down to investigate, and red squirrels come to scold human visitors. One might inadvertently flush a ground-dwelling ruffed grouse, triggering a noisy explosion into the air, an experience as unnerving for the hiker as it is for the bird. Occasionally the forest opens on to a glacial pond. Ospreys often nest around such water and are easily seen. Five Ponds offers hikers a glimpse of how the whole region looked centuries ago.

One of the most intriguing projects of the Nature Conservancy, which has saved many rare ecosystems in the Adirondacks, is the **Gadway Sandstone Pavement Barrens Preserve❖,** west of the Canadian border town of Mooers Forks. During the last ice age, an enormous chunk of what is now northern New York and southeastern Canada was covered by a vast glacial lake named Iroquois, the ancestor of Lake Ontario. About 12,000 years ago, the water breached a wall holding the lake and a colossal deluge ripped over the land, a cataclysmic flood. The geologic record indicates that within a few weeks a huge amount of water—many times greater than any flood documented in historical times—was released, and the lake surface dropped 80 feet.

In this area just shy of the Canadian border, the flood tore away existing vegetation and scoured soil from bedrock. It left behind a huge rippling "beach" of pinkish Potsdam sandstone, now known as a sandstone pavement barren. Fewer than 20 such sites exist around the world. Over 10,000 years, the barrens developed a unique ecosystem: a forest of jack pine, scruffy trees of twisty, gnarled profiles like the fantasy trees in a Disney movie. Visiting the barrens has been likened

ABOVE: *An aquatic feeder, a bull moose spends summers on his own; in fall he mates with a series of cows, which give birth the following spring.*

to a walk through a bonsai forest because the pines, although 120 years old, are only five to six feet tall. Their dwarfism results from the meager nutrition available in the mere three to six inches of soil covering the bedrock and also from the inability of the substrate to absorb water during the summer growing season. Substandard nourishment is also responsible for a minimal understory in the "bonsai forest." The plants that do grow, such as lowbush blueberry, chokeberry, and black huckleberry, prefer very acidic conditions. Along the edges of the forest, where there is more soil, the jack pines grow taller.

THE CHAMPLAIN VALLEY

Some Adirondack attractions are privately owned. One of the most popular is **Ausable Chasm**❖ on Route 9, 12 miles south of Plattsburgh. Approximately 500 million years ago, this area was a seafloor where layer after layer after layer of mud, muck, and sand slowly accumulated. Once drained and dried, this ancient ocean bottom hardened into Potsdam sandstone. Millions of years later, as the last of the ice ages waned, meltwater created a modest river, the Au Sable. Find-

LEFT: *In a rocky cove at Point au Roche park on Lake Champlain, purple loosestrife and cottonwood trees absorb the rays of the setting sun.*

ing a crack in the sandstone bedrock, the glacial runoff started channeling and after 10,000 years produced an impressive gorge.

Today the Ausable begins life timidly as drainage from Mount Marcy and pinnacles in the High Peaks and travels only 50 miles to its ultimate destination, Lake Champlain. By the time it reaches the gorge, however, it is a high-volume, high-velocity river roaring between multi-tiered walls of sandstone rising 100 to 150 feet above the churning water. At some spots the walls are only 30 feet apart. The layered cliffs frequently flow and curve in riverine fashion, without sharp angles; at other points the stone has been "chiseled" into multiple mini-blocks.

Visitors make the first half of the 1.5-mile journey on foot, frequently encountering rock formations that erosion has carved into surprisingly recognizable shapes—"elephant head" and "pulpit rock," for example. There are no plunging waterfalls in the chasm, just a hot-rodding river. The last half of the tour is by boat on a channel between tall cliffs barely 20 feet apart. The craft negotiates two mild white-water rapids and a whirlpool that provides quick thrills but is unlikely to cause injury.

Lake Champlain❖ stretches 120 miles between New York and Vermont, ranging in width from a quarter mile to 12 miles. In New York it is most attractive some 30 miles south of Plattsburgh around Essex, where in 1994 the state added 1,826 forested acres and 3 miles of lakeshore to Adirondack Park. The parcel includes **Split Rock Mountain,** only 1,125 feet tall but wide open to glorious views of the High Peaks to the west and the lake and Vermont's Green Mountains on the east. Another appealing perspective can be had from the deck of the ferry that plies the waters between Essex and tiny village of Cedar Beach, Vermont, near Vergennes.

THE HIGH PEAKS

Visitors can walk or drive up **Whiteface Mountain❖,** which boasts one of the most magnificent vistas in the Adirondacks. Situated at the edge of the High Peaks area, Whiteface affords 360-degree views of at least a

LEFT: *From sun-dappled Whiteface Mountain, Lake Placid shimmers in the twilight. Whiteface owes its contours to long-departed glaciers.*
OVERLEAF: *Bulrushes pervade a luxuriant Connery Pond near Lake Placid as the majestic bulk of Whiteface looms above the morning mist.*

LEFT: *A common loon and chick nest on a pristine lake. George Washington Sears, an Adirondack traveler in the 1800s, described the loon's echoing cry as "clearer than a clarion, sweeter than a flute."*
RIGHT: *A secluded pond near Whiteface could be the forest primeval, where nature's cycles proceed undisturbed. As ghostly conifer trunks decay, new growth springs up to take their place.*

dozen of its lofty neighbors, among them Mount Marcy, highest of the high (Whiteface is fifth in line at 4,867 feet). The mountain acquired its name when an early-nineteenth-century landslide produced an enormous scar of milky white anorthosite, a relatively rare rock.

The Whiteface Mountain Veterans Memorial Highway (off Route 86) leads within 700 feet of the bald, windy summit, and from there visitors can take an elevator or a trail to the top. Aside from peaks, fine views feature Lake Placid, Lake Champlain, and the Vermont countryside. On a really clear day, Montreal is visible up the Saint Lawrence.

A few miles west on Route 86 is another nature-based commercial attraction, **High Falls Gorge❖.** Near its source in the High Peaks, the Au Sable River races ten miles through Wilmington Notch. Narrowing to its tightest passage, the gorge forces the river into a frantic froth as it twists and turns between sheer granite walls—gray, blue, even pink—boiling around boulders and long, slim stone dikes that divide the stream in spots. Like a granite-bound shoot-the-chutes, the cascade plunges more than 600 feet over three levels of falls to a boiling pool below.

In 1791 Thomas Jefferson wrote: "Lake George is, without comparison, the most beautiful water I ever saw; formed by a contour of mountains into a basin thirty-five miles long, and from two to four miles broad, finely interspersed with islands, its water limpid as crystal, and the mountainside covered with rich groves of thuja [hemlock], silver fir, white pine, aspen, and paper birch, down to the water edge." The present-day **Lake George❖** remains the queen of all the Adirondack waters, a long, slender sapphire-blue designer lake and one of America's grandest.

Scientifically speaking, Lake George is an oligotrophic dimictic

LEFT: *Dawn illuminates the considerable splendors of Lake George. The quintessential Adirondack lake, its deep, clear waters lie in a slim boulder-strewn valley flanked by steep mountains.* **RIGHT:** *A pair of great horned owls provide a striking contrast. The dark owl at right, with large ear tufts and a white neck collar, is a full-grown adult; its nondescript companion is still immature.*

lake—a deep body of pure clear water rich in oxygen that turns over twice a year. It owes its crystalline clarity to a combination of factors. Because it is mostly spring-fed from below, relatively little organic matter flows into the lake. Depths ranging to 190 feet keep it cold as well as clear. And an aquatic plant called *Nitella,* or stonewort, grows in meadows on the lake bottom 20 to 40 feet down, filtering out sediment and organic matter that could cloud the water. Regrettably, clarity is threatened by lakeshore development, which leaks pollution into the water, clouding it and robbing *Nitella* beds of sunlight essential to their cleansing activities. Conservationists are working on the problem.

There are several ways to see Lake George. Fifty miles of hiking trails provide a series of mountainside views. Cruise boats weave among the 225 wooded islands dotting the lake's 150,000 acres of liquid surface. In a six-mile-long corridor called the Narrows, islands are densely concentrated in an especially fetching jigsaw puzzle of woods and water. The Veteran's Memorial Highway ascends Prospect Mountain for perhaps the most spectacular views of the lake and adjacent countryside, which on a clear day can stretch well into Canada.

RIVER AND GULF

In the Adirondack wilds, water is a dominant theme; assuming myriad guises, it links all the other elements. A case in point is the **Upper Hudson River** and **Upper Hudson River Gorge❖.** The Hudson originates in Lake Tear of the Clouds, a sort of mucky puddle in the wetlands near Mount Marcy's summit. Slowly it becomes a river, albeit narrower and

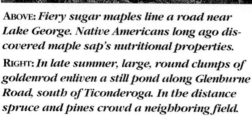

ABOVE: *Fiery sugar maples line a road near Lake George. Native Americans long ago discovered maple sap's nutritional properties.*

RIGHT: *In late summer, large, round clumps of goldenrod enliven a still pond along Glenburne Road, south of Ticonderoga. In the distance spruce and pines crowd a neighboring field.*

wilder than the one that flows past Albany and New York City.

A trail to the "young" Hudson begins off a bumpy dirt strip called Northwoods Club Road, reached from Route 28N near Newcomb. A fairly level, five-mile round-trip, the trail leads through dense forest where wildflowers make a crazy quilt in spring. The route concludes opposite Blue Ledge, a 300-foot steel-blue granite cliff that reflects even bluer in a deep pool at its base—the deepest, most picturesque part of the Hudson Gorge. In spring the river is supercharged by snowmelt as well as water from tributary streams, a genuine gee-whiz spectacle as it surges along its narrow course between canyon walls rising more than 300 feet straight up from the water's ferociously roiling surface.

Adventurous travelers prefer to experience the Hudsonian turmoil by raft. Trips depart from Indian Lake on Route 28, traveling south to the village of North Creek, a frenzied 17-mile ride through almost continuously "boiling" water in a walled canyon where rapids ratings reach IV and V, comparable to Rocky Mountain rivers. As though it

had been rudely awakened from a long winter's sleep and was mad as
hell, the Hudson rockets past Blue Ledge, OK Slip Falls (a 250-foot
splash—tallest in the Adirondacks), and other cascades and landmarks.
It travels through remote wilderness unreachable by any other
method—awesomely rugged terrain where eagles sometimes soar
overhead in solitary splendor and bears peer down from cliff tops.
Bathed by water only a couple of degrees above freezing, rafters are
kept busy fending off deadly boulders while trying to avoid being
swamped by waves that can tower 18 feet tall.

   Just outside the park's western boundary at the edge of the
Adirondack foothills lies the Tug Hill Plateau, a remote, rough-hewn
region of small mountains, narrow gulches, and swampy flatlands.
Although few people live here and not many come to visit, there is
one good reason to go: **Whetstone Gulf State Park❖,** on Routes
12D and 26 just north of Houseville. Gulf is a term used hereabouts
for ravines with extremely steep walls, and Whetstone fills the bill.

ABOVE: *White pines and balsams line the edge and various hardwoods hug the bottom of the precipitous ravine at Whetstone Gulf State Park.*

This abyss can inspire awe of natural forces, provoke dizzy spells, or trigger nightmares about free-falling. Along its three miles, the walls at most spots drop 385 feet to the bottom. It appears much deeper because it is so narrow—only a few feet across at the ends—and the walls are so steep that they verge on vertical.

Composed of slim slabs of shale and siltstone—thousands of them—the walls seem to vibrate as sun and shadow spill over their sides. Between the multiple planes of charcoal to blue-black rock near the top are bands of sandstone, a type used locally as whetstones to sharpen knives—hence the place name. A five-mile trail follows both sides of the ravine's rim north and south for breathtaking (literally) views almost straight down. Visitors can also explore the gulf's flat bottom on a three-mile trail beside a creek that rushes through the pass. Postglacial waterfalls cut this groove, and a waterfall still plunges 50 feet at the head of the chasm.

RIGHT: *A bright swath of wildflowers, including pink joe-pye weed and yellow goldenrod, blanket the verge of a country road near Whetstone.*

PENNSYLVANIA

PART TWO

PENNSYLVANIA

W illiam Penn was a paradoxical plutocrat: a member of England's seventeenth-century landed aristocracy yet also a radical nonconformist. His passionate religious convictions earned him expulsion from Oxford University and a prison sentence in the Tower of London. So when Penn asked King Charles II to repay a £16,000 loan made to the monarch by Penn's father with a land grant in the new American colonies, His Majesty was delighted to dispose of both a large debt and an annoying gadfly. In 1681, the crown issued William a charter for Pennsylvania, which means "Penn's Woodlands," and the young rebel landed there the following year.

Penn received a large roughly rectangular colony nearly the size of the state's present 45,333 square miles. Most of it was—and is—mountainous. More than 80 percent of the state is contained within two vast geologic provinces. The largest, the Allegheny Plateau, is a collection of little flattop mountains, including the Poconos, and valleys. Glaciers deepened the valleys and added further refinements in the state's northeastern and northwestern corners. When the glaciers retreated, numerous streams eroded and crosshatched the landscape. On a topographic relief map, the plateau makes a sweeping north-to-southwest C-shaped arc toward Maryland, dominating the western part of the state.

Immediately to the south of the plateau is the Valley and Ridge Province, where a series of long curving ridges parallel one another like a giant accordion, alternating with broad, flat valleys. This washboard topography is the result of a devastating collision of the tectonic plates composing the earth's crust that occurred 300 to 220 million years ago. The Valley and Ridge Province follows the same east-to-west flow, curving from the Delaware River to the Maryland border except for a finger poking north into the plateau. The remainder of the state—the southeastern corner—is a geologic potpourri, predominantly Piedmont, a rolling land of plump green hills

---

PRECEDING PAGES: *West of the Susquehanna River, just north of Harrisburg, the Tuscarora Mountains rise in a series of curving ridges.*

and rich soil. In pristine condition prior to 1600, nearly all the state was covered by some of the richest mixed forest east of the Mississippi.

Before European settlement, the virgin land was home to indigenous peoples, some 15,000 Iroquois, Susquehanna, Shawnee, and Delaware. Swedes established a colony in 1643, only to be ousted in 1655 by the Dutch, who were in turn uprooted by the British in 1664. Once William Penn claimed his territory, he pronounced Pennsylvania a Holy Experiment dedicated to individual freedoms, especially of religion. Such liberty, along with rapid economic growth, lured streams of settlers in the 1700s. English, Welsh, and Dutch Quakers began filling the eastern counties. Slightly to the west, rich farmland drew Rhineland Germans, nearly all of them members of persecuted religious sects: Amish, Mennonites, Moravians, Dunkers, and Schwenkfeldians, known collectively as Pennsylvania Dutch. Scotch-Irish immigrants began to populate the state's western frontier.

In the nineteenth century, agriculture expanded throughout the southeastern wedge while in other parts of the state a wealth of natural resources —oil, coal, natural gas, iron ore, and other metals—were harvested, an exploitation that severely scarred the land as well as polluting the air and water.

In the twentieth century, Pennsylvania began cleaning up its environment and even regreened large chunks of abused habitat, such as Moraine State Park, just north of Pittsburgh. When the state acquired that land in the 1950s and 1960s, it was a developmental disaster, site of more than 400 oil, natural gas, and water wells, plus both pit and strip coal mines. By capping wells, cleaning away debris, and restoring the forest, Pennsylvania produced a model of reclamation. Founded in 1893, the state parks system now administers 116 parks covering more than 277,000 acres. About two million more acres are protected in state forests and another million in state game lands. The parks alone provide more than a thousand miles of trails.

Nongovernmental outfits also helped. The Western Pennsylvania Conservancy, headquartered in Pittsburgh, has purchased numerous sites, managing some and placing others under state protection. In eastern precincts, the Pennsylvania chapter of the Nature Conservancy has performed a similar service. Smaller, specialized groups—notably the internationally renowned Hawk Mountain Sanctuary—have also played vital roles.

As the twenty-first century approaches, tourism is second only to agriculture among the state's industries. Although many travelers are drawn to Pennsylvania by historic shrines, thousands also come for its estimable natural attractions. After 300 years, the state can take pride in the knowledge that William Penn would probably still recognize the place.

EASTERN PENNSYLVANIA:
POCONOS TO PIEDMONT,
DELAWARE TO SUSQUEHANNA

Every autumn, tens of thousands of migrating hawks and eagles navigate a southbound course through the eastern third of Pennsylvania, an area roughly defined by the Delaware River on the east and the Susquehanna River and Route 15 on the west. Riding winds and air currents, the birds soar over the Great Valley, which curves casually from the Delaware toward the Maryland border. From their lofty perspective, the overall landscape north of the valley is obviously greener than that to the south. People are scarcer in the northeast, relatively speaking, and fewer highways lace the terrain; whereas the dense network of roads in the southeast suggests that a congregation of drunken spiders drew the road map.

The state is dominated by two enormous geologic provinces that occupy more than 80 percent of the land: the Allegheny Plateau and the Valley and Ridge Province. Roughly equal portions cover the northeastern area of the state, with the plateau curving over the northern end along New York. Despite its name, the plateau's topography is hilly because it was dissected by a battery of streams, then scoured and sculpted by glaciers into deep chasms and lush wetlands. Farther south, the Valley and Ridge Province is a series of curving, parallel ridges of upthrust sedimentary rock that lay flat over most of the state millions of years ago. During an era of colossal tectonic plate collisions between 300 and 220 million years ago, the megaforce released caused rocks to

LEFT: *In Bowman's Hill Wildflower Preserve on the Delaware River, white snakeroot flourishes beside Little Meadow Trail. Juice from this plant's leaves was once believed to counteract the toxic effects of snakebite.*

buckle and thrust upward into folds, producing this wrinkled land-scape. Separated by wide, fertile valleys, the sharp-edged ridges double back on themselves, rippling over the land like waves in a sea of stone. In this "Vista City," scenic overlooks dot the ridgetops. Also within the undulating stonescape are spectacular water gaps and wind gaps, mountain passes where streams have sliced through tough, resistant rock. (Wind gaps began as water gaps, but the streams that engineered them deserted the projects.)

The less populated northeast attracts large numbers of temporary inhabitants through its primary attractions, the Pocono Mountains and the Delaware Water Gap. The wooded, mountainous scenery has spawned a cottage industry based on family resorts and honeymoon hideaways featuring heart-shaped hot tubs. Separating north from south, the Great Valley is the most intensely folded part of the Valley and Ridge Province; but its lowlands are pockmarked with caves and sinkholes, products of porous limestone and dolostone. At the lower edge of the Great Valley begins the Piedmont, a hilly land that ripples south to Georgia. Because the soil is good, farms occupy most of the space between cities in the area called Pennsylvania Dutch country.

Anchoring the south, metropolitan Philadelphia, which has almost six million people, is one of America's megacommunities. It occupies part of the narrow strip of pancake-flat coastal plain that runs along most of the eastern seaboard. The route for this chapter begins in Philadelphia and its suburbs and swings west to Lancaster and the Susquehanna River. It then angles northeast to the Delaware Water Gap and finally explores the picturesque Poconos.

PHILADELPHIA AND ENVIRONS

If birds filed flight plans, observers would look askance at a plan that listed Philadelphia as its destination. The birds know what they are doing, however, when they head for the **John Heinz National Wildlife Refuge❖,** on Lindbergh Boulevard at 86th Street, in the city's densely populated, heavily industrialized southwestern corner. Locat-ed within spitting distance of the runways of an international airport and rimmed on the south by heavily trafficked I-95, the preserve is nevertheless a key location on the Atlantic Coast Flyway.

Originally called Tinicum, the refuge contains multiple habitats

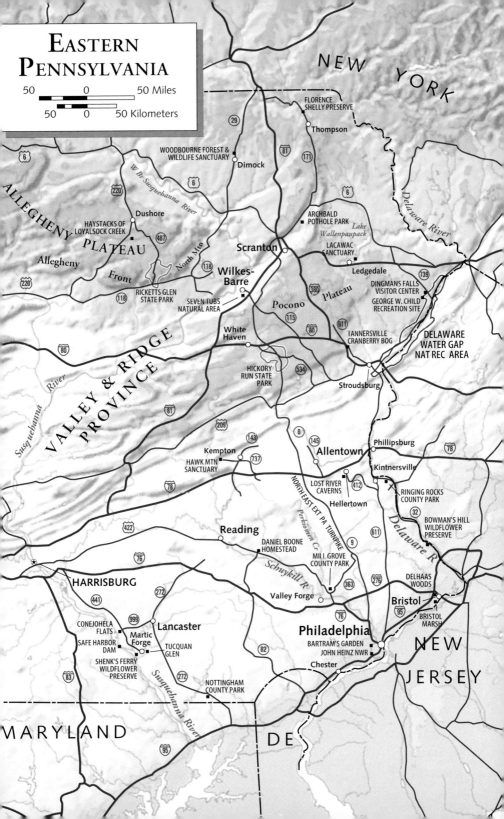

within its 1,200 acres: a 205-acre freshwater tidal marsh (the heart of the refuge), a large pond impounded by dikes, smaller ponds, a tidal creek, and upland forest. Each year thousands of birds descend on this wetland. Some 288 species have been tallied, mostly waterfowl and shorebirds. Ducks, sparrows, and red-winged blackbirds swarm to feed

on a variety of marsh plants that sway and caress the edges of vast pools of water, while shorebirds probe broad, shimmering mudflats bubbling with tasty invertebrates.

Within the grasses, sedges, and rushes, more than 85 species nest, including Virginia and king rail, least bitterns, marsh wrens, and northern harriers. Populations of these marsh-dependent species have declined throughout the northeastern United States, and refuges like this one are critical to their long-range survival. A large heron rookery is the nesting mecca for four different species. In some years, such shorebird rarities (for this part of the world) as ruffs, American golden plover, and Wilson's and red necked phalaropes pause in their travels. During spring and fall, hundreds of warblers and other songbirds mob the woodlands. Those seasons are the best times to visit, not only because migrants are abundant but also because biting bug populations are modest to nonexistent.

Above: *The red-winged blackbird's distinctive, resplendent shoulder patch is sometimes hidden when the bird is at rest.*

Left: *At the John Heinz refuge, a boardwalk bisects a pond lit by the emerald sheen of floating duckweed. Waterfowl find this plant delectable.*

Closer to Center City on the west bank of the Schuylkill River, at the intersection of Lindbergh Boulevard and 54th Street, is the nation's oldest surviving botanical garden. Historic **Bartram's Garden❖,** a 44-acre park set amid factories and oil refineries, is one of the best places in the country to sample America's native flora.

John Bartram (1699–1777), a Quaker farmer and self-taught naturalist-botanist, began tilling this land early in the eighteenth century. He soon departed from standard agriculture in order to collect and cultivate wild plant specimens. He and his son, William (1739–1823)—a devoted tourist, diarist, and natural-history artist—traveled extensively: north to the shores of Lake Ontario, west to the Ohio River, south to the Carolinas, Tennessee, Mississippi, Louisiana, Georgia, and Florida. Returning each time with seeds and cuttings, they grew specimen plants and created a "garden of inquiry," eventually transforming the collection into what we now call a commercial nursery and publishing America's first plant catalog.

ABOVE: *William Bartram painted this water-color of* Franklinia alatamaha, *a native flowering tree. Luckily he saved seeds from a tree he saw in Georgia in the 1770s; by 1803 the species was extinct in the wild.*

RIGHT: *Bartram's Garden features a tall yel-lowwood tree and many flowers, such as fleabane, goldenrod, phlox, and cleome.*

Although the garden today is about half its original size, there is plenty to see at the restoration, which follows John Bartram's plans as closely as possible. Some of the most intriguing specimens are trees and shrubs, and among the rarest is Bartram's Oak, a naturally oc-curring hybrid of red and willow oaks that the naturalist discovered on his own land. Among the oldest trees is a sprawling 50-foot-tall yellowwood sent from Tennessee or Kentucky by French botanist André Michaux more than 200 years ago. Each May, long racemes of creamy white flowers drench its aging boughs. The most celebrated tree is one that John and William discovered in Georgia in 1765 and named Franklinia (*Franklinia alatamaha*) to honor their good friend Ben Franklin. By 1803, all these trees had disappeared from the wild, and they exist today only because of the Bartrams, who saved an

ABOVE: *In Bowman's Hill preserve, the shiny red foliage of a sourwood tree contrasts with nearby greenery. In early summer, the tree produces white, urn-shaped flowers resembling lily of the valley blossoms.*

endangered species more than two centuries before the concept existed. The Franklinia's white camellialike blossoms, centered with sunbursts of golden stamens, perfume the park in late August and early September.

About 19 miles north of Philadelphia in suburban Bristol, the Nature Conservancy has preserved one of Pennsylvania's best remaining examples of a freshwater tidal marsh, one that rises and falls each day to help cleanse the Delaware River. Although surrounded by commercial development, **Bristol Marsh❖,** an 11-acre wetland, supports six rare, highly specialized plants that have all but disappeared from the state, among them waterhemp ragweed, Walter's barnyard grass, and two species of arrowhead. A productive nursery for aquatic life, the marsh is also a safe haven for migrating waterfowl.

A short drive north in Bristol, a portion of Silver Lake County Park known as **Delhaas Woods❖** is a remnant of the coastal-plain forest that once covered most of present-day Philadelphia. Another rare ecological community, Pennsylvania's only coastal-plain bog, also survives here. Although the land was once heavily farmed and logged, the preserve contains the state's densest concentration of plants native to coastal-plain forests. In spring the big fleshy, creamy white blossoms of umbrella and sweet bay magnolias still lend southern charm to the understory. The forest harbors more than a dozen rare and endangered plant species, a predominantly purple group that includes Maryland meadow beauty, eastern blue-eyed grass, and long-leafed aster. The star tree on the premises is a 200-year-old willow oak whose trunk measures 14 feet around.

Farther north along the Delaware is the site where one cold December night George Washington made a strategic crossing of the river (standing heroically in the front of the boat only in Emanuel Leutze's famous painting of the event). Within **Washington Crossing Historic Park❖,** two miles south of New Hope on Route 32, 80-acre **Bowman's Hill Wildflower Preserve❖** allows visitors to view wild flora from all over Pennsylvania. Farmland and pasture in the late nineteenth century, this slice of the Pidcock Creek valley has reverted to youthful second-growth forest. The people who established Bowman's Hill in the 1930s and 1940s preserved and managed—manipulated really—the mildly hilly terrain to encourage some 1,500 species of native wildflowers, shrubs, trees, ferns, and vines to grow. To accommodate the specialized needs of plants that would not normally thrive here, they also created artificial environments, making some plots dry and others wet, some soils sweet and others acid.

Today the mosaic of woodlands, bogs, ponds, meadows, and barrens appears totally natural and wild. Twenty-six different trails focus attention on specific plant and habitat types. One, for example, is devoted to plants used for medicinal purposes, another to ferns (30 varieties in six different habitats), another to alien plants that have become naturalized. One path winds exclusively among azaleas and their relatives, while another concentrates on the holly family. Although the preserve is open year-round, the season is March through early October, and spring is an especially showy time.

Artistic inspiration abounds around **Mill Grove, The Audubon Wildlife Sanctuary❖,** in Philadelphia's western suburbs at the intersection of Audubon and Pawlings roads (off Routes 363 and 422) near Valley Forge. This Montgomery County historic site was the first American home of John James Audubon, who was installed by his father as resi-

dent manager of a 175-acre farm and lead mine on Perkiomen Creek in 1803. America's best-known wildlife artist first sketched birds here, noting in his diary: "Its fine woodlands, its extensive acres, its fields crowned with evergreens, offered many subjects to my pencil. It was there that I commenced my simple and agreeable studies, with as little concern about the future as if the world had been made for me."

Virtually unchanged since Audubon was in residence, Mill Grove is ideal for communing with both birds (181 species recorded, of which 60 are known to nest here) and flowers (more than 400 plants cataloged). Stand by the veranda of the ivy-covered manse and peer upward to the top of an oak, where in spring Baltimore orioles flash like orange flames while tending their pendulous, baglike nests. House wrens dart about the lower levels, flicking upright tails before popping in and out of tiny nest holes. Bolts of blue skipping above the lawn are eastern bluebirds scurrying into nest boxes. A stroll down a long, grassy slope to the creek may provide a view of wood duck parents guiding a fluffy, golden new brood. Wander woodland paths to enjoy the silvery fluting of a wood thrush and an occasional glimpse of the speckle-breasted bird.

Just outside Philadelphia's western limit about five miles south of Montrose on Route 29, the Nature Conservancy's **Edward Woolman Nature Preserve❖** encloses a wetland area that was never heavily settled and thus escaped the usual destructive by products of human habitation. Today the largest freshwater marsh in eastern Pennsylvania, the preserve features a 400-acre marsh, a submerged meadow lush with cattails, tall grasses, and a variety of shrubs. More than 200 flowering plants have been identified in the refuge. The larger Canadian Saint-John's-wort—starlike with five bright yellow petals in summer—reaches the southern end of its range at Woolman and grows in only one other Pennsylvania location. More than 155 bird species find the marsh appealing; 30 warbler species alone stop during migration. Also present are a couple of rare butterflies, the black dash and the mulberry-winged skipper. This fragile and beautiful spot may be visited only on guided tours conducted by the Nature Conservancy.

*LEFT: **This classic portrait from Audubon's** Birds of America **depicts three Baltimore orioles in a tulip tree (yellow poplar). The black-capped birds are adult males; a gray-backed female guards the hanging nest.***

PENNSYLVANIA DUTCH COUNTRY

About 25 miles southeast of Lancaster, **Nottingham County Park❖** off Route 272 is world famous for its serpentine barrens. Serpentine is a light green stone that appears in only three areas in North America: California and southern Oregon, Canada's Gaspé Peninsula and western Newfoundland, and astride the Mason-Dixon line in southeastern Pennsylvania and northern Maryland. It originated deep under ocean bottoms eons ago, and only occasionally have the plates of the earth's crust moved in a way that thrust the stone through the surface. Quarrying has been actively pursued, and in Chester and neighboring counties green farmhouses, churches, and other buildings faced with serpentine dot the countryside. Fortunately, some outcrops have been preserved in this 651-acre park.

The serpentine here is an olive shade that deepens to black in spots. The stone fosters unique communities of plants, many of them low-growing but colorful. In April hordes of moss pinks—in three different shades—cluster in rock crevices and along the edges of the outcrops. Inconspicuous except for its small five-petaled pink blossom, the round-leaved fameflower is a rare succulent adapted to this dry, rocky environment. The short reddish, nearly leafless stalks of serpentine asters appear nowhere else in the world but these barrens and an area across the border in Maryland. Their white daisylike flowers bloom in late summer and early autumn.

Botanical splendor of a very different sort envelops visitors to **Shenk's Ferry Wildflower Preserve❖,** off Route 324 close to the Susquehanna River, roughly a 12-mile drive south of Lancaster. In this woodsy ravine near Pequea, the alkaline limestone soil provides the kind of nutrition that encourages wild flora to go *really* wild. Show time is primarily a spring affair. Between mid-March and mid-May, the spectacle features an all-star cast of more than 60 wild species. In mid-April, Virginia bluebells and white trilliums carpet entire hillsides. Blossoming continues through summer and early fall in the 30-acre refuge, where more than a hundred species have been identified.

On River Road, about four miles south of Martic Forge, **Tucquan Glen❖** is a little gem known to surprisingly few citizens of nearby Lancaster. The trail follows crystalline Tucquan Creek for a little more than a mile through a narrow wooded ravine of multilayered schist cliffs flecked with moss and lichens. For two thirds of the way, the stream is a peaceful, barely rippling waterway winding through a shady medley of nearly pristine forest, primarily tall black birches, tulip trees, and eastern hemlocks. More than 40 tree species grow in the glen, as do more than 40 wildflower species and 21 kinds of ferns (3 of them rare), which create little pocket gardens amid a rippling carpet of mosses and ground pines. The glen is delightful year-round, but on a hot summer day the dense shade makes it a particularly welcome oasis.

As it nears the Susquehanna River, the creek gathers steam, whipping between walls of rhododendrons and hemlocks, surging around enormous moss-covered boulders, and churning itself into a series of rapids, waterfalls, and plunge pools. Visitors who wish to follow it must wade over shallow spots several times, so waterproof boots—or a tolerance for wet feet—are advised. Having worked itself into a frenzy, the creek subsides into flatness again and gurgles peacefully into the river.

Near where Route 999 (west from Lancaster) intersects 441 is a refuge right *in* the Susquehanna, **Conejohela Flats,** a major migration layover site on the eastern flyway. Conejohela is actually a chain of three fairly large wooded, brushy islands with connecting mudflats, which appear and disappear daily as the Safe Harbor Dam raises and lowers water levels. This wet habitat lures close to 30 shorebird species and waterfowl by the ton (25 duck species alone), as well as gulls, terns, herons, ibises, loons, grebes, and cormorants. During March and April the flats are inundated by waterfowl. In March thousands of tundra swans pause on their way north, sometimes joined by thousands of snow geese. From late April through May, shorebirds blanket the muck. During August six species of southbound swallows dart and dash through the air like feathered bullets. Bald eagles nest about three quarters of a mile south of the flats in spring and summer. For variety of species, autumn (through mid-November) is the choicest time. Although the islands are off-limits from March 1 through July 31, visitors may view the birds from the shore with a spotting scope or from a boat with binoculars. The mudflats may be visited anytime they are above water (boots advised).

ALLENTOWN VICINITY

Along an angled northeastern route toward the Delaware, natural and cultural history merge north of Route 422 about six miles east of Reading at the **Daniel Boone Homestead❖.** Boone was born here in 1734 and

127

Each fall, thousands of migrating raptors ride the warm air currents above the curving ridges below Hawk Mountain (right). Major species include the majestic Cooper's hawk (above); the somewhat smaller sharp-shinned hawk (below left); and the even smaller American kestrel (below right), which combines a songbird's plumage with the beak and talons of a bird of prey.

128

lived on the property 16 years. In addition to seven historic pioneer-era buildings on this 600-acre plot, two nature trails wind through woodlands like those where the great frontiersman first became acquainted with nature.

Every fall, two kinds of transients—both numbering in the tens of thousands—congregate near the small village of Kempton. Their objective is the **Hawk Mountain Sanctuary❖,** about seven miles west of the intersection of Routes 737 and 143. Earthbound transients flock here to observe airborne travelers—birds of prey migrating south from eastern Canada, New England, and New York to the southern United States, as well as Central and South America.

Air currents shaped by mountain ridges—like the Kittatinny, where the 2,200-acre refuge is located—channel and propel southbound birds along a sort of aerial highway. As the sun heats the air near the earth's surface, the air expands into gigantic bubbles called thermals. The bubbles rise, drawing cooler air from a north-facing ridge. Buoyed by thermals, hawks ride the currents, expending very little energy, until the bubbles cool and dissipate. By that time the birds have climbed aboard another bubble. The ridge's topography also attracts the hawks. When the season's prevailing northwesterly winds smash against a ridge's flank, they shoot up and over the ridgetop, forming an updraft that lifts and pushes the birds along. On a good day, a hawk riding air currents at an average speed of 40 miles per hour can travel more than 250 miles.

Thus wind, weather, and terrain conspire to concentrate great numbers of hawks and eagles into a relatively narrow corridor, creating one of America's greatest wildlife spectacles—a sort of avian Serengeti. On average, 20,000 birds of 14 species are tallied during the four months of migration. On a crisp, clear day when the winds are right, hundreds of raptors—on magical days, thousands—sail past Hawk Mountain. Dozens may barrel into view all at once.

The experience is almost always best at the North Lookout, about a three-quarter-mile hike from the road. Roughly 1,500 feet above sea level, this rise overlooks a patchwork of fields neatly plowed by Pennsylvania Dutch farmers and woodlands gaudy with fall foliage colors. Humongous slabs of grayish Tuscarora sandstone splotched with gray-green lichens are tumbled about randomly, forming a promontory that pokes like the prow of a ship into an ocean of airspace. The panoramic view sweeps around the point, so birds can be tracked for miles. When the northwesterlies are truly whipping around, the birds press close to the ridgetop to escape turbulence. The intimate views of soaring hawks that birders enjoy can be awesome.

Migration begins with a trickle in the last half of August, swells into big numbers in September, continues heavy through November, and peters out in mid-December. One of the first species to appear is the broad-winged hawk, master of thermal transportation. Often big flocks of broad-wings appear in mid-September, swirling around inside thermal bubbles in a phenomenon called a kettle. Bald eagles also favor September travel.

Accipiters—principally sharp-shinned and Cooper's hawks, but also some goshawks—prefer October. A distinctive flying style—flap, flap, flap, glide—distinguishes these small gray-backed woodland hawks. Red-tailed and red-shouldered hawks, also most numerous in October, tend to glide high with outstretched wings on helpful air currents. These buteos continue strong into November, when golden eagles are most likely to soar majestically overhead. As a general rule, October provides the greatest variety of species. The best days are those when a cold front has passed through and reasonably strong northwesterly winds are rushing past the mountain.

Among the many tourist-oriented caves in the region, **Lost River Caverns❖,** off Route 412 in Hellertown, just southwest of Allentown, merits a visit. As in all such enterprises, the owners have given free rein to their imagination when naming the more intriguing stalactites, stalagmites, and other formations. One expansive flowstone at Lost River shimmers red, pink, yellow, cream, white, and other mineral-produced colors as it blankets stone walls with multiple folds that suggest a church interior. Called the Crystal Chapel, the chamber is indeed frequently used for nondenominational wedding services.

At **Ringing Rocks County Park❖,** off Route 32 about ten miles south of Phillipsburg and some three miles east of Kintnersville, the curi-

---

OVERLEAF: *In Hickory Run State Park, large boulders fill a vast clearing— roughly the size of 30 football fields—amid dense evergreens. The stones are a legacy of the glaciers that once covered much of North America.*

ous may want to seek an assembly of boulders that emit chimelike tones when tapped with a hard object. Iron combined with other minerals inside the rocks is the source of sound. Bring a hammer, but tap lightly.

THE POCONOS

Between 20,000 and 10,000 years ago, glaciers shaped the eastern end of the Allegheny Plateau, known as the Pocono Plateau, leaving behind an array of geologic curiosities and a potpourri of wetlands. Most sites along this northern tier have a glacial heritage. South of I-80 near White Haven, **Hickory Run State Park❖** on Route 534 features a national natural landmark called the **Boulder Field.** Suggesting labels like "moonscape" or "dreamland," a vast, jumbled heap of modest-to-enormous boulders stretch across a forest clearing 1,800 feet by 400 feet. Most rocks are less than 4 feet in diameter, but many exceed 26 feet in length. Although the bottom of the pile is invisible, geologists have determined that it is at least 12 feet deep. Because the stones absorb sounds made by visitors and wildlife, an eerie silence envelops the scene, as if hundreds of stone sarcophagi—some rounded, some sharply angled, according to the whims of erosion—had been cast adrift in an alien world.

Depending on the amount of sunlight, a soft reddish haze covers the rocks, which range from red sandstone on the north end of the field to red conglomerate pebbled with white quartz on the south. The boulders were once part of nearby ridges to the north and south. When water seeped into fractures in the ridges, then froze and expanded, huge blocks of stone were separated from the mother rock and tumbled into a talus slope at the base of the ridge. During the waning centuries of the last ice age, 20,000–18,000 years ago, thawing and freezing of the earth repeatedly stirred sand, clay, gravel, and ice, mixing this debris with the boulders and inching them farther down the slope into a valley. When the glacier retreated for good, the weather warmed and meltwater drained the refuse. Except for the forest that grew along its perimeter, the stony spread is locked in time, an ice age relic that looks as it did thousands of years ago.

Farther north on the plateau, just south of I-80, is the Nature Conservancy's **Long Pond Reserve.** This unique ecological patchwork of scrub oak–pitch pine barrens, heaths, wetland forests, bogs, and little vernal ponds is home to more than 10 rare plant species and hordes of

ABOVE: *Cranberry Creek winds through boreal forest in the Tannersville Cranberry Bog. Amid mats of sphagnum, native cranberry vines produce pink blooms in June; the fruit they bear in summer ripens by autumn.*

butterflies and moths (at least 15 species of these insects qualify as rare). The 15,000-acre preserve protects 40 threatened plant and animal species and natural communities, and 7 of those are rated vulnerable throughout the world.

Always interesting, Long Pond truly dazzles in the third week of May, when a wild native American azalea (*Rhodora canadense*) blooms, casting a reddish purple glow over vast stretches of the barrens and heaths. This very fragile place is closed to the public.

The colossal glaciers that occupied northern Pennsylvania shaped the landscape in many ways. The last one left behind, among other things, huge buried blocks of ice crusted with sandy, rocky debris. When the ice melted about 14,000 years ago, a hollowed-out basin in the eastern Poconos became a 715-acre kettle lake that eventually became a bog. Kettles have no inlets or outlets and are sustained primarily by rainwater. Lacking aeration from flowing streams, they are low in oxygen, producing an environment high in acid and low in nutrition.

The glacier also imported seeds of plants living much farther north, and spores of sphagnum moss, which found that conditions here suited it splendidly. Over thousands of years, the moss crept over the lake's surface. Eventually a dense floating mat six inches thick became the foundation of the **Tannersville Cranberry Bog✧**, off Route 611 about five miles northwest of Stroudsburg. Wetlands occupy about 400 of the preserve's 1,000 acres, and the bog is its 150-acre centerpiece.

Atop the soggy green carpet is a forest that resembles a slice of wilderness transported from Canada or the Adirondacks and is very different from the oak-maple woodlands around the bog. The sphagnum, a vast sponge that during summer slowly evaporates water, acts as a natural air conditioner to cool its surroundings into a microclimate. The insulating moss keeps ice from thawing until June, creating a boreal or northern bog. This low-altitude boreal bog is the southernmost along the eastern seaboard. The plant community typifies cold-climate habitats. For instance, cotton grass, a sedge with a wispy white puff at the end of its stem, normally grows only in latitudes much farther north.

Like sphagnum, black spruce and tamarack, the dominant trees in the bog, are glacial imports. Beneath the moss mat lies not soil but decaying vegetation—peat—that is totally saturated with water. Near the edge, the bog is 30 feet deep; at the center, 60 feet. In many spots, decomposing fern fronds, sedges, and other plants have mounded on the sphagnum to create small lumpish islands that are not saturated. Although trees and shrubs root on these hummocks, the absence of oxygen and nutrition inhibit growth so much that a small tree may be a hundred years old.

A 1,450-foot floating boardwalk makes the bog accessible to visitors, but it may be seen only on guided tours conducted by the Monroe County Conservation District. Despite the impoverished environment, the sphagnum mat is a raft of life, a botanically rich floating garden crowded with acid-loving plants and shrubs that blossom throughout spring and summer. The most abundant bloom and color appear the third week in June with wild callas, rose pogonia, sheep laurel, yellow loosestrife, bog laurel, and insect-eating pitcher plants. June is also flowering time for cranberries, which grow on vines and are smaller than the commercially harvested bush-type berries. The bog copper, a rare purplish-brown butterfly, feeds on the nectar of the cranberry's small pale-pink blossoms and lays its eggs exclusively on this plant.

After following a plethora of billboards on Route 209 northwest along the Delaware and wading through knee-deep commercialism at the entrance, travelers enter exquisite countryside along **Bushkill Falls❖.** The Poconos are cascade country, and here Bushkill Creek launches a downhill sprint through a ravine that transforms the stream into a variety of falls. The main falls drops a hundred feet through a wide cleft between solid sheets of sandstone edged by moss and wall-hugging trees and shrubs. Actually a series of moderate to fairly long plunges (with a few smaller bumps in between), the falls gather white threads into a broad, deep pool where the water swerves around a sharp corner and shoots downward again. Several wooden staircases provide visitors with scenic options, each route descending and ascending steep chasm walls and frequently spanning the churning stream.

THE DELAWARE WATER GAP

Loosely speaking, a water gap is a place where a river cuts through a series of mountains instead of flowing alongside them. Aided and abetted by faults, uplift in the mountains, and erosion, the Delaware River chiseled its path through the tough, resistant sandstone and conglomerate of Kittatinny Ridge. Many miles south of its Catskill Mountains origin in New York, the Delaware widens and deepens, then sweeps in a tight S curve through forested mountains as it shoots the gap. Long before I-80 ripped through the area, the gap was a popular vacation spot and a favorite subject for artists, particularly members of the Hudson River School. More than a century later, the U.S. Park Service has preserved 70,000 acres straddling 40 miles of the river as the **Delaware Water Gap National Recreation Area❖.** Because the Delaware hereabouts is a relatively calm stream ideal for canoeing, the site attracts four million visitors a year.

Although some of the NRA's acreage is farmland, most remains in a natural, if not virgin, state. Some 200 miles of roads facilitate motorized exploration, and miles and miles of trails invite those who prefer to do their discovering on foot. A reasonably level trail from the **Dingmans**

OVERLEAF: *At the summit of Mount Tammany a striking view of the rugged Delaware Water Gap unfolds, with Mount Minsi rising on the Delaware's western bank. The national recreation area extends 40 miles upriver.*

Left: *A common but welcome sight in winter, a gray squirrel pauses to reconnoiter. The frosty granules on its snout suggest that it has been rooting in the snow, hoping to scent a buried nut.*

Right: *The Delaware is fairly placid as it slices through Kittatinny Ridge, but nearby Dingmans Falls provides a thrilling display of falling water.*

Falls Visitor Center❖ twists through a forested ravine deeply shaded by hemlocks, many more than 300 years old. The path follows rusty red Dingmans Creek, colored by tannin leached from the hemlocks' craggy bark. The sharply angled ravine walls are mostly shale, a soft multilayered gray stone. Ferns, shrubs, even small trees cling to chinks between layers in this natural hanging garden.

Around a bend, the slender, sparkling strand of Silver Thread Falls drops 80 feet through a narrow cleft. A little farther on, the broader, taller waterworks of Dingmans Falls cascade down 135 feet over half a dozen blue-gray tiers, sending thick sheets of water outward. On the final drop, hissing water sprawls over a long tilted plane of rock, creating a sort of bumpy water slide. The stream concludes with a spin around a clear rock-walled pool inhabited by trout.

A short drive northwest off Route 739, another "aquacade" provides the centerpiece of **George W. Child Recreation Site❖,** a section of the recreation area. Here Dingmans Creek metamorphoses through three waterfalls. The first stop is Factory Falls (named after a woolen mill built next to the water in 1825). After dropping a couple of feet, the creek makes a sharp turn and separates into myriad hairline traces to take a long dive over a wedge-shaped precipice. By the time it circles some stone basins, it has fallen about 60 feet.

At Fulmer Falls, water seems to spray from several "spigots," traveling in wide and narrow pathways and plunging with colossal splashes at each of several steps down. According to legend, the third cascade, Deer Leap Falls, honors a cornered stag that preferred taking its own life to being shot by a Native American hunter. Hugged by forest, the stream seems to burst from the vegetation and plunge, creamy and frothing, until it shatters over a broad rock dome about 30 feet below.

Calming down, it drifts on to a rendezvous with rocks at Dingmans Falls, farther down the slope.

Westward in the Poconos next to Lake Wallenpaupack near Ledgedale, the **Lacawac Sanctuary❖** lies at the end of a meandering three-mile drive north from Exit 6 of I-84. Its glory is a 52-acre "ice scour" lake that glaciers carved in the shape of a hook. Because its incredibly clear water distinguishes it as the southernmost unpolluted glacial lake in North America, Wallenpaupack is the focus of considerable scientific research. Within nearly 500 acres, the reserve contains swamps, marshes, meadows, ponds, a quaking bog, and a second-growth hardwood-conifer forest. Black bears and other large animals inhabit these woodlands, but visitors are more likely to spy tiny orange and green newts skittering amid the leaf litter.

Glacial engineering produced another superlative in the area: the world's biggest pothole. Off Route 6, six miles northeast of Scranton, the irregularly shaped **Archbald Pothole❖** (in a 150-acre state park of the same name) measures 38 feet deep with diameters ranging from 24 to 42 feet.

Botanical superlatives characterize the **Florence Shelly Preserve❖,** on Route 171 two miles north of Thompson in the state's northeastern corner. This 358-acre wetland wonderland is a compact assemblage of boreal bog, both upland and swamp forests, a 10-acre glacial pond, wet meadows, cattail marshes, and bubbling springs. It nurtures more than 375 vascular plant species, including a bevy of delicate orchids. Aficionados will also find a flock of plants of lower orders, among them 14 kinds of sphagnum moss.

The largest virgin forest in northeastern Pennsylvania survives in the **Woodbourne Forest and Wildlife Sanctuary❖,** one mile north of Dimock on Route 29. About 200 of the reserve's 648 acres shelter old-growth hemlocks and a hardwood mix of mostly beeches and red maples, plus red oaks, yellow and black birches, sugar maples, white ashes, and black cherries. Hemlocks a hundred feet tall and more cast deep shadows on the forest floor. Most are two to four centuries old, and at least a few approach 500 years. Within the forest, a 16-acre alder swamp supports 85 plant species, including a dozen kinds of fern. The surface of Cope Pond is dotted with floating islands of sphagnum, where bog plants like sundew and pitcher plant (both insect eaters) grow in the moss. Wildlife is plentiful and noteworthy for tiny gems: nine salamander species, including purple, two-line, and four-toed. A short nature trail travels through part of the virgin forest and along the swamp's edge, but some areas—the pond, for instance—may be visited only with special permission.

Glacial evidence sometimes suggests a human ability to think and create, as if the icy masses had experimented with art forms while grinding back and forth. Such a phenomenon is the **Seven Tubs Natural Area❖,** a Luzerne County park on Route 115 on the southern outskirts of Wilkes-Barre. There glaciers carved a ravine (Wheelbarrow Canyon), and when the last ice flow abandoned the site about 14,000–12,000 years ago, its meltdown generated a torrential stream of water that swept through the gorge, transporting tons of debris, from monstrous boulders to grains of sand. At several points along the crevasse, the water spun and smashed glacial garbage so violently that it gouged a series of deep basins—tublike potholes—from the bedrock sandstone and conglomerate. Estimated at 18–22 feet deep, the largest tub has a diameter of 15 feet; but no one has been able to measure the depth of the basins accurately.

Wheelbarrow Run, as the stream is known today, slices down the wooded slope through a narrow notch of rock in a series of furiously frothing falls. The stream strikes a pool, swirls around making modest waves, and then swings away to plummet to the next depression. In many spots, the glistening rock walls enclosing the water are rounded in big, graceful curves as though smoothed and burnished by giant hands.

If visitors had to limit themselves to a single natural site in eastern Pennsylvania, the obvious choice would be a wilderness fantasy of cascading waters and soaring trees called **Ricketts Glen State Park❖.** About 22 miles west of Wilkes-Barre at the junction of Routes 118 and 487, the park straddles the Allegheny Front, a steep escarpment where the Allegheny Plateau meets the Valley and Ridge Province. Millions of years ago, streams began eroding a Y-shaped gorge in the bedrock. Glacial abrasion deepened it, and debris-laden meltwater completed

OVERLEAF: *A rough-hewn trail ascends toward Harrison Wright Falls in Ricketts Glen State Park. At their peak in spring, the park's spectacular cascades showcase Kitchen Creek as it hurtles through the steep terrain.*

LEFT: *In a luxuriant summer meadow, a white-tailed doe washes her spotted and spindly six-day-old fawn. If the deer are pursued by a predator, the mother's white tail patch will help the fawn to keep her in sight.* RIGHT: *A secluded trail passes through a gallery of towering hemlocks in Ricketts Glen. Left undisturbed, hemlocks can survive for many centuries.*

the sculpting when the glaciers departed 15,000–10,000 years ago. Today two branches of Kitchen Creek rocket down North Mountain, the west fork tearing through Ganoga Glen, the east branch through Glen Leigh. The wedge is the **Glens Natural Area,** a registered national natural landmark. The streams join at Waters Meet and continue south through Ricketts Glen. The full course drops about a thousand feet in 2.3 miles, along the way producing a catalog of cascades: 22 waterfalls significant enough to be named, plus a host of anonymous falls splashing down the ravine walls.

This aquatic extravaganza occurs in a shadowy virgin forest where hemlocks and white pines mix with beeches, oaks, maples, and other hardwoods. Many of the trees measure nearly five feet in diameter. Among these giants, an age of 500 is not unusual, and most are at least 200. Although the forest is magnificent, the water display is the park's most spectacular feature. Falls range in height from 11 to 94 feet, most clustering in the 30-to-40-foot range. In "wedding cake" formations, water tumbles down a series of sandstone stairs, and in "bridal veils," hard gray sandstone caps softer rock, such as red shale, that has eroded faster, leaving a projecting sandstone lip that causes water to drop in sheets. Sometimes the two styles combine. Every one is distinctive.

Starting at the top of Ganoga Glen, for example, Mohawk Falls plunges 37 feet in three stages. After splashing over multiple stairs, the stream curves around to a second drop, gliding over rocks green with moss carpets. At the lowest level it swerves back and forth, boiling as

146

it descends six wide steps. The next cascade, Oneida, is a near-solid sheet of water, barely separated into quarters as it falls 13 feet. Cayuga is split by a stony projection, bouncing over mossy stairs on one side, dropping as a watery curtain on the other, an 11-foot jump into a wide plunge pool. Ganoga, the tallest at 94 feet, stutters and shatters down innumerable steps, curving slightly and gradually widening as rivulets rain into a shallow basin. In addition to the architecture of the falls, the ever-shifting streambed, massive boulders and layered ledges, potholes, and forest arching over the stream provide an infinite variety of perspectives. Spring—when snowmelt swells the falls to their peak flow of the year—is a favorite time to explore the glens, and lots of water still flows in autumn, when fall foliage colors the landscape even more dramatically.

West of the glens, the Loyalsock Trail wanders 57 miles along the path of Loyalsock Creek. Off Route 220 about 6 miles south of Dushore, a portion of the trail follows an old railroad bed to the **Haystacks of Loyalsock Creek❖.** About a mile off the highway the path through hemlock forest meets a short trail that leads to Loyalsock Creek, which whips through a seemingly extraterrestrial landscape. Rising from the streambed are large domed boulders reminiscent of the moguls that Olympic skiers bounce over to win medals. These weathered humps of tough sandstone—the Haystacks—were formed when the stream eroded softer rock. The formations now modify the creek into a series of small pools and mini-rapids.

WESTERN PENNSYLVANIA:
THE APPALACHIAN UPLANDS

Except for the interstates, driving the roads of western Pennsylvania is like riding a roller coaster. The experience can be especially unnerving early in the morning, when clouds snuggle into valleys. With visibility verging on zero, travelers must negotiate an unending battery of curves, loops, bends, hairpins, and long, steep inclines. Periodically the road emerges from the cottony blanket into gray light, crests a hill, and plunges into the miasma once more. Later, when the atmosphere clears, the roller coaster remains.

The rugged rising-and-falling terrain explains why the state's western two thirds beyond Route 15 are wilder and—relatively speaking—less developed than the eastern third. Although a couple of large industrial cities flourished here, the landscape discouraged the agriculture, settlement, and extensive highway construction that characterizes the east.

About 65 percent of the western region is wrapped in the geology of the Allegheny Plateau—even though the landscape doesn't look much like a plateau. Over some 200 million years, rivers and streams cut through the bedrock, slicing it into flattop hills crisscrossed by deep, narrow valleys. During the most recent advance, from 20,000 to 10,000 years ago, glaciers etched and gouged more features into the northwestern sector. No mountain giants rise here—the tallest is a tad

---

LEFT: *Hemlocks, witch hazel, and cinnamon ferns border Kildoo Run in McConnell's Mill State Park. Kildoo's rocky ravine was created at the end of the last ice age when glacial lakes overflowed into nearby valleys.*

more than 3,200 feet—but enough hills cluster tightly together to give highway engineers fits.

The rest of western Pennsylvania also presents rugged up-hill-down-dale terrain, but the rhythm is different. Southeast of the plateau is a chunk of the Valley and Ridge Province, an accordion fold of long, sharp-edged ridges paralleling one another. Valleys here are wider and flatter. And massive rock layers jut upward sharply in vertical and diagonal configurations, a decided departure from the plateau, where rocks layer horizontally. The only other exception to plateau dominance is a slim strip of lowland along Lake Erie in the state's northwest corner.

Although the rough-and-tumble landscape slowed development, the spectacular wealth of natural resources above and below the surface made exploitation inevitable. In the late nineteenth and early twentieth centuries, fortunes were made by plundering timber, oil, natural gas, coal, iron, and other minerals. But the industrial boom carried high price tags: scarred and denuded landscapes, air and water pollution, and a general decline in wildlife.

Today's visitors, however, see few signs of the area's industrial past. The inevitable dwindling of natural resources and the spirit of environmental reform combined to give the forces of nature a fighting chance. Once more, magnificent forests rise from the hills in second-growth, sometimes third-growth, splendor, and a few scraps of ancient forest endure. The water in the small streams that streak and slip through the mountains is much cleaner than it was a half century ago; some never were polluted. Locally these rocky little waterways are usually called runs, rarely creeks.

Western Pennsylvania has always been a botanical bonanza, a region where southern and midwestern wild plant species reach the ends of their ranges and mingle with eastern species. Because the paths of aerial migration pass through the area, similar diversity characterizes bird populations.

The chapter exploring Pennsylvania's wild west begins smack in the

---

OVERLEAF: *In late August, Meadow Trail in Raccoon Creek State Park is alive with wildflowers. Yellow goldenrod and black-eyed Susans, white Queen Anne's lace, and purple ironweed crowd the narrow pathway.*

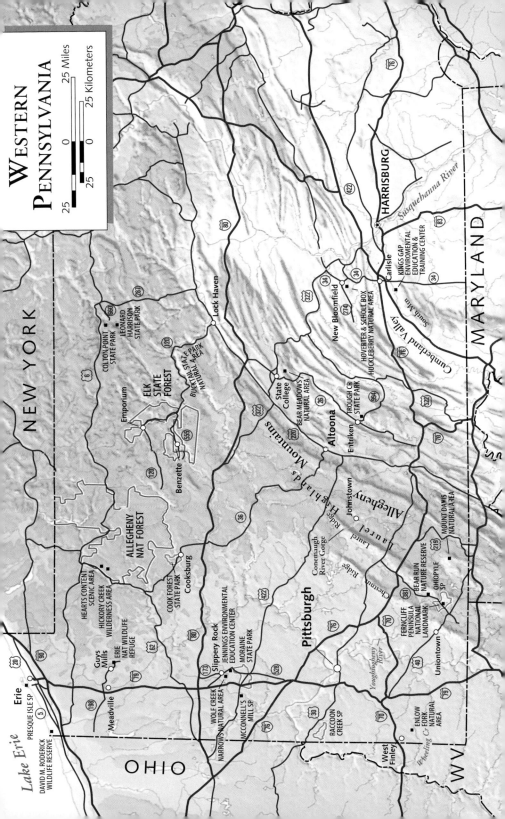

center of the commonwealth at State College. It travels south over rippling ridges, west into the Laurel Highlands, then due north through Pittsburgh to Erie. The final leg weaves eastward among vast upland forests to conclude at Pennsylvania's version of the Grand Canyon.

IN THE HEART OF THE VALLEY AND RIDGE PROVINCE

Almost within earshot of the cheers resounding from the football stadium that is the den of the perennially powerful Nittany Lions of Penn State lies a habitat with no business in this neighborhood. To reach it, travel southeast from State College on Business Route 322 for 5.8 miles to Bear Meadows Road, the turnoff for the Tussey Mountain Ski Area, and continue south 4.8 miles to **Bear Meadows Natural Area❖** in **Rothrock State Forest.** Occupying a basin of more than 500 acres that is circled by ridges 500 to 600 feet higher, the natural area traps heavy, dense cold air from the mountains, creating a microclimate in the bowl.

ABOVE: *In early autumn, the scarlet fruits of a winterberry shrub contrast with fading marsh grasses at Bear Meadows Natural Area.*

LEFT: *Because of an unusually cool microclimate at Bear Meadows, balsam firs and black spruce are rapidly advancing from the periphery of a watery sphagnum bog.*

Temperatures here are significantly cooler than in the surrounding countryside, and thermometers may register freezing (or lower) nine months of the year.

Although the edges of the basin are forested, its core is a boreal bog, a plant community more at home well to the north and in Canada. At first glance, the landscape suggests the work of glaciers, but the nearest glacier stopped 60 miles northeast. The much earlier geologic turmoil that produced the folded terrain also left behind a bedrock bowl. Probably beavers—or a landslide—dammed a stream running through this bowl, allowing sphagnum moss to move in. Ultimately moss and other decaying plant life filled the depression with a seven-foot layer of peat.

155

The grassy path to the bog traverses rings of mixed oak and white pine–hemlock forest enlivened with tall tangles of mountain laurel (glorious in mid-June bloom) and rhododendrons (resplendent in early July). An observation platform provides an overview of the open wet-

land, which looks more like a wet meadow as Sinking Creek (the primary drainage) curves quietly through it. In the woods around the perimeter, springs bubble up and direct small streams into the wetland.

Up close the bog is a mat of sphagnum and sedges sprinkled with starflowers, goldthread, corn lilies, cotton grass, several orchid species, tough little insect-eating sundews, and such acid-loving shrubs as bog laurel, leatherleaf, viburnum, and highbush blueberry. Along the bog's southern edge grows a cool Canadian forest of black spruce and balsam fir (rare in Pennsylvania) that is, ever so slowly, filling in the mossy mat. Many of the plants and shrubs are spring bloomers, but mid-July through August means ripe blueberries.

How small can a small gem be? Try a nine-acre patch of dry woods north of Carlisle. This heavily shaded, west-facing slope is the **Hoverter and Scholl Box Huckleberry Natural Area❖,** a national natural landmark that is home to one of the rarest of native shrubs. Also one of earth's oldest living organisms, box huckleberry has been found on only a handful of isolated sites in seven states, the six others all south of Pennsylvania. To explore this worthwhile but obscure reserve, travel southeast from New Bloomfield 1.5 miles on 274/34 to an unnamed intersection. Turn left (south) and after about 600 feet, left again on Huckleberry Road. The site is half a mile farther on the left; watch for the sign, which tends to blend into the woods.

ABOVE: *A 1,300-year-old growth of the rare box huckleberry shrub extends over nine acres at the Hoverter and Scholl natural area.*

Box huckleberry is an attractive but subtle plant, a mini-shrub ground cover. Stems arch gracefully upward from the forest leaf litter, the largest only six to eight inches tall. Oval leaves of deep, waxy forest green that resemble boxwood (hence the name) alternate on either side of slender stems. Rarity is only part of the plant's story. The entire colony, covering nearly nine acres, is a single plant. It spreads by extending runners, adding about six inches a year and taking more than a thousand years to blanket this site. Botanists estimate that it is 1,300 years old, possibly even older. The best time to appreciate the plant is May and June, when its bell-like blossoms—some white, some blushing to pink—appear. Next best is July and August, when light blue berries arrive. They disappear quickly because ruffed grouse consider them a great delicacy.

Ten miles south of Carlisle is a 1,454-acre state park dedicated to a specific mission. **Kings Gap Environmental Education and Training Center❖,** on Pine Road off Route 34, is a mountainous, wooded "classroom" that emphasizes organized nature study for schoolchildren (through college level), teachers, and civic groups. Casual visitors are welcome too. A long winding drive up South Mountain leads to park headquarters and a sweeping vista of forest and farmlands in the Cumberland Valley.

ABOVE: *Combining delicate pink blossoms with sturdy limbs, the evergreen mountain laurel is Pennsylvania's official state flower.*

Kings Gap's 15-mile network of hiking trails wind through a variety of habitats, including an oak and pitch pine forest, its understory marked by blueberry and huckleberry bushes; a pine plantation; a maple forest supported by fertile soils and abundant moisture; a white oak forest; and a chestnut oak forest, which thrives in drier conditions and predominates throughout Kings Gap. A small pond and stream, home to painted turtles and spotted salamanders, is surrounded by wetland vegetation such as skunk cabbage, tulip trees, and cinnamon ferns. Reptile denizens include state-threatened timber rattlesnakes, copperheads, and five-lined skinks (lizards). The area's extensive educational activities utilize this wealth of

habitats. The park was originally designed as a summer estate by a member of the Cameron family of nearby Harrisburg.

The heart of **Trough Creek State Park❖,** on Route 994 about 15 miles southeast of Altoona and some 5 miles east of Entriken, is a deep, narrow ravine clothed with hemlocks and rhododendrons that cling to nearly vertical slopes. This gorge is typical of those that slice through the Valley and Ridge Province, except that its rocks are layered horizontally, the opposite of the usual configuration in the area. Geologic curiosity is the 541-acre park's strong suit. A trail following a stream through the ravine leads to Balanced Rock (also called Raven Rock), a very large boulder perched improbably at the edge of a cliff. When the creek carved its valley, this block of sandstone separated from cliffs and edged its way downslope as other rocks in front of it eroded away. It has remained there for thousands of years and apparently is not going anywhere soon.

The Laurel Highlands

In the southwestern corner of Pennsylvania three low ridges dominate the landscape. Remains of much larger folds in sedimentary rock from millions of years ago, they are—looking east to west—Allegheny Mountain, Laurel Ridge, and Chestnut Ridge. Collectively they form the Laurel Highlands, the most thinly populated part of the state. The ridges have eroded into masses of hilly projections that seem packed together in especially high density.

The best place to sample the Laurel Highlands' scenic splendor is **Ohiopyle State Park❖,** on Route 381 southeast of Uniontown. This large park (19,000 acres) was once a hunting ground for the Iroquois, Shawnee, and Delaware, who dubbed the area Ohiopehhelle (meaning "water whitened by froth"). The Youghiogheny River, which chops a 1,700-foot-deep gorge 14 miles through Laurel Ridge, winds through the park. The Indian name Yohoghany means "a stream flowing in a roundabout course." The name is pronounced Yock-uh-gay-knee, and the river is usually called the Yough (rhymes with *rock*).

LEFT: *Below the falls of the Youghiogheny River, in Ohiopyle State Park, rafters (center) tackle challenging rapids. The densely wooded flanks of Laurel Ridge frame the river throughout its exhilarating journey.*

Frothy water on a winding course is one of Ohiopyle's principal attractions. At the park's hub (visitor facilities, shops, outfitters), the river flows over Ohiopyle Falls, a sweeping 20-foot drop carrying a greater volume of water than any other cascade in Pennsylvania. A series of rapids follow. Many visitors are content simply to admire the photogenic wild river, where more adventurous sorts enjoy some of the best white-water rafting in the eastern United States. The Middle Youghiogheny, which contains gentle class I and II rapids at normal water levels is for novices who want a float trip with some easier white water, not a wild ride. The Upper Yough offers awesome class V white water strictly for experienced rafters. Just below the falls, the Lower Yough is a serious affair; the class III and IV rapids can fling people and boats tail over teakettle if sensible rules are not observed.

A white-water expedition on the Lower Yough is a bumpy, even tricky, ride. At first, after the rafts are launched, the trip seems like a peaceful glide between two tall green walls. On a sunny spring day, catkins and dandelion fuzz rain from above, and the river's rushing, rippling sound in the distance barely breaks the silence. Quickly, however, the volume builds to a near-deafening roar, and rafters are pulled and bounced through Entrance Rapid, a series of ledges, giant boulders (including a monster called Sugarloaf), and sprinklings of large, extra-rough rocks stirring three-foot waves. As the raft careens around this stony curve, powerful crosscurrents and eddies yank it about brutally. When the river is high, the rapids are class IV, otherwise class III. At either level, dry clothing is only a memory after encountering the river head-on.

Rafters barely have time to catch their breath before Cucumber, an area just below the entrance of Cucumber Run into the Yough, where plunge follows plunge at high speed with no time to think, only to fend off menacing boulders. Underwater boulder gardens (as rafters call them) whip up waves and create holes in the surface to make the trip more interesting. Challenges come in rapid succession: Piddly, Camel, Walrus, Eddy Turn, Dartmouth—all random designs of colossal lumps of 500-million-year-old Pottsville sandstone. Repeatedly smacked and bashed by churning water, the raft is tossed about, tipped side to side, washed with gallons of river. Often the boat shoots upward, then crashes with a resounding smack, only to take to the air again in a fraction of a second. And sometimes the vessel spins 180 degrees from the direction the paddlers had in mind. After 7.4 miles, rafters suddenly realize that the sport is tremendous fun for anyone who is physically able.

If water touring doesn't appeal, 41 miles of trails beckon hikers to explore on foot. **Ferncliff Peninsula❖,** a national natural landmark, is a 100-acre sandstone knob that forces the river to curve around it in an oxbow. Dense thickets of rhododendrons and mountain laurel crowd the inner edge of the path around the rocky rim; great views of river and falls open on the other side. Several trails meander through this botanically rich site where northern and southern forest ecosystems overlap. As it flows north from Maryland and West Virginia, the Youghiogheny transports seeds, enabling southern species to extend their range into the north. Buffalo nut, for instance, is a parasitic shrub that grows on the roots of other shrubs and trees. Its alternate name, oil nut, comes from the large oily, poisonous seed inside yellow-green fruit that ripens in summer. Other southerners include Carolina tasselrue (or false bugbane), slender blue iris, and autumn willow. The rarest of the lot is large-flowered marshallia, which is scarce everywhere and grows in Pennsylvania only at Ferncliff. Sprouting from rocky crevices along the river, its showy lavender, sometimes pink, blossoms—similar to bachelor buttons—open in June.

For fairly serious trekking, Ohiopyle State Park is the southern terminus of the **Laurel Highlands Hiking Trail❖,** which runs nearly 70 miles along Laurel Ridge, through mixed hardwood forests, to a trailhead near the Conemaugh River Gorge just west of Johnstown. About 30 miles east of Ohiopyle is the **Mount Davis Natural Area❖** off Route 219, which contains the highest peak in the state (3,213 feet). Mount Davis also merits the distinction of being the *lowest* high point in the Appalachian states. Nevertheless, on clear days it offers pleasant views of the countryside.

Although the western slope of Laurel Ridge has been logged and farmed, after many decades a large chunk of it has been reborn as a wild place. In the 5,000 acres of **Bear Run Nature Reserve❖** on Route 381, 19 different trails total more than 20 miles, wandering mainly through oak and hemlock forests. At some points huge groves of rhododendrons arch over the trail to form tunnels; in early July they're bright with thousands upon thousands of pink and white blossoms. The trails follow and repeatedly cross Bear Run, a spirited stream that

ABOVE: *White large-flowered trillium (top left) graces eastern woodlands in early spring. The* **Rhododendron maximum** *(bottom left), or great laurel, is a stately evergreen shrub that can grow to 20 feet.*

rushes frantically and noisily through the woods, occasionally subsiding to a bubbly murmur as it swirls around a trout pool before dashing off on another sprint over mossy boulders. In April and May, wildflowers such as trailing arbutus and painted trillium are everywhere.

Tucked into the southwestern corner of the state, a stone's throw from West Virginia, the 914-acre **Enlow Fork Natural Area❖** is a sleeper of a site that no nature lover should miss. The title refers to a branch of Wheeling Creek; officially the preserve is known as State Game Lands 302. Despite its isolation, the land was worked in bygone years, but today relatively little evidence of the farming and logging remains.

The natural area is in a rural section where road signs—either verbal or numerical—are scarce. From the village of West Finley, turn south at a T intersection toward Graysville. Go 2.8 miles to Burdette, where an iron-and-wood-plank bridge crosses the creek. After crossing the bridge, drive 1.7 miles up a modest incline on a dirt and gravel road. A

ABOVE: *This clearing in the Enlow Fork Natural Area is alive with yellow-flowered goldenrod and pink clusters of joe-pye weed. Birds and insects thrive here as well, pollinating new generations of plant life.*

dirt road intersects at a sharp angle on the right (it's easily missed), and a barely visible sign reads "State Game Lands." Follow that road downhill until it ends at a grassy parking area by an old washed-out bridge.

From the parking area, follow the ruts of an old road past a meadow that was once a cornfield and up a modest slope. In May myriad melodies brighten the surroundings as migrating and nesting birds flit among the trees and grasses—Baltimore orioles, wood thrushes, yellow-shafted flickers, yellow warblers, red-winged blackbirds, scarlet tanagers. At the peak of the slope, the remnant road swings left abruptly. The wooded slope to the left is a wild garden of coral-colored columbines with yellow centers, blue cranesbill, tiny white wild ginger, vivid scarlet fire pinks, deep blue larkspurs, and blue phlox. An uncommon tree, the yellow oak (also called chinquapin oak), grows around this bend in the road. Except for its flaky light-gray bark, it resembles chestnut oak.

The path travels downhill, and on the wooded slope a quiet walker may hear the rustling of a rufous-sided towhee scrabbling in leaf litter for insect food, a spooked chipmunk scurrying to a hiding hole, or a very chubby groundhog noisily exploring, sometimes excavating, the turf, indifferent to tourists. Visitors may also spy a silent box tortoise, frozen in mid-motion, trying to be invisible in the tall grass. About halfway down the slope, a bluish haze amid the dappled light of open woods is evidence of blue-eyed Mary, a wildflower species from the Midwest that is rare in Pennsylvania.

At the bottom, the road hangs a right and crosses a bridge over the creek. Beyond, blotchy-barked sycamores dominate the flood plain. A fallen tree supports a winding staircase of shelf fungi. Within this area are buckeye trees (usually a southern species) with cones of golden yellow blossoms. A few feet farther, the floor of the open woodland becomes a lavender blue tapestry woven and snugged around the trunks of sycamores and elms, occasionally oaks and maples—blue-eyed Mary at its most glorious. Numerous patches in the tapestry's weave are accented by other shades of blue or purple: Virginia bellflowers, cranesbill, and blue phlox, with occasional flecks of white trilliums complemented by the deep greens of the plants' leaves. On the opposite side of the rutted trail, rock ledges and limestone outcrops have become fern gardens.

Although early May may be the primest of times, April is also grand for forest wildflowers. The summer months yield a different array of plants, including another rarity, Riddell's hedge nettle, a rosy purple blossom on hairy stalks. Resident birds and nesting migrants—and their new offspring—remain plentiful until late summer. The enormous butterfly population swells in spring and explodes into greater visibility as summer arrives and the wealth of wildflower nectar provides a feast for the gaudy insects.

PITTSBURGH TO ERIE

The names Pittsburgh and Erie do not evoke images of natural magnificence. Yet on the edges of these large industrial cities, and along I-79 between them, a near-legendary assembly of flora and fauna awaits. Only 25 miles west of downtown Pittsburgh on Route 30 is **Raccoon Creek State Park❖,** a hilly, wooded haven of more than 7,300 acres. Its star attraction is the **Wildflower Reserve,** occupying 314 acres at the eastern tip, which supports more than 500 wildflower species. From late March through early October, something is in bloom; peak season is usually early May.

A combination of factors produce the bounty of blossoms here. Although some of the area was farmed, most of it escaped development. The reserve also encompasses a diversity of ecological habitats: floodplain, meadow, oak-hickory and beech-maple forests, a pine plantation, shale cliffs, and varied topography at several elevations. Finally, at this spot on the map the regional ranges of numerous plants converge and overlap, making the botanical potential much richer than it would be a hundred miles farther east.

Half a dozen trails meander through the habitat conglomerate. One path near the nature center traverses a tree-identification section, then winds down a cliff past clumps of Virginia bluebells, whose clusters of lavender bells droop from slender stems during early May. In the flat valley at bottom, a heavy tree canopy cloaks the land in ragged shadows, pierced here and there by theatrical pinpoints of sunlight. For a while the path edges Raccoon Creek, a gurgling stream where brownish gray eastern phoebes shoot from tree limbs to snatch flying insects. Hikers are surrounded by sounds and sights of birds: tufted titmice, scarlet tanagers, downy and red-bellied woodpeckers. On this route at the base of the bluff and along the stream, botanical bounty reigns in patches of blue woodland phlox, dwarf larkspur, rose-purple cranesbill, blue cohosh, yellow trout lilies, Solomon's seal, jack-in-the-pulpits, and five types of trillium. In the wooded floodplain near the juncture of two trails, great drifts of asterlike golden ragworts sweep between the trees.

A very different display appears in late summer, when the meadow blossoms with green-headed coneflowers, black-eyed Susans, scarlet cardinal flowers, lavender blue closed gentians, wingstems with drooping skirts of long yellow petals, and several sunflower species. At the Wildflower Reserve, repeat visits are in order.

Closer to the northwestern part of the state, glacial remnants begin to cram the landscape as they do in the Northeast. During the last glacial epoch, giant ice sheets dammed Muddy Creek and Slippery Rock Creek, forming a lake system north of present-day Pittsburgh. When the ice retreated about 20,000 years ago, lake meltwater spilled into a valley, undammed the creeks, and cut a 400-foot-deep ravine. **Slippery**

LEFT: *Shaded by a leaning silver maple, the 1874 Mc-Connell's Mill Bridge spans mist-shrouded Slippery Rock Creek. The state has some 200 covered bridges, the most in the country.*

RIGHT: *Velvety mosses and polypody ferns (a mat-forming species that grows on rocks, banks, and trees) flourish in the woodlands along the Kildoo Trail in McConnell's Mill State Park.*

Rock Gorge is the heart of **McConnell's Mill State Park**❖, on Route 422 about 40 miles north of Pittsburgh and 1.7 miles west of I-79.

Hell's Hollow Trail, in the western end of this fragmented park, follows Hell Run, a tributary of Slippery Rock Creek, along a shadowy path. In late April and early May, crowds of spring beauties and wild blue phlox greet hikers. Among deeper shadows, both red and white trilliums flower in extravagant numbers. At one point the stream passes through a flume—a half-oval trough 80 feet long and 5 feet deep—created by a limestone overhang that is sprinkled with wild columbines. Most of the time Hell Run is a trickly little creek, but near trail end, it bursts through a layer of limestone into a 19-foot waterfall, countless threads of liquid gliding down a lumpy stone slide into a shallow pool. It continues—although the trail doesn't—another 250 feet down the slope to merge with Slippery Rock Creek.

The most remarkable thing about **Moraine State Park**❖ is that it exists at all. Located on Route 422 east of I-79, it is a shining example of nature reclaimed and resurrected. Only a few decades ago, this land was severely scarred by more than 400 oil, natural gas, and water wells, plus both pit and strip coal mines. All those had to be cleaned up, the wells securely capped, and the land restored to a semblance of its original green, forested state. The park's centerpiece is Lake Arthur, a seven-mile-long reproduction of a glacial lake that existed here 20,000 years ago. Today's handsome lake is about two thirds smaller than the original.

Thanks in large part to glaciers, a small segment of western Pennsylvania looks like Kansas. Around the town of Slippery Rock, melting

167

*Blazing Star Trail at the
Jennings center (right) is
an outdoor wildflower
museum showcasing
prairie flora. The dense
purple blazing star
(above) is the jewel of the
collection, but the golden-
hued oxeye (below), is
equally dazzling. Although
seemingly dissimilar, both
belong to the aster family.*

glaciers turned basins into lakes about 14,000 years ago. Over several centuries sand, silt, and clay particles settled to the lake bottoms. When the ice—and the lakes—vanished, they left about six inches of soil. For thousands of years, the region's climate drifted back and forth between hot and cold. Some 7,000 years ago, it turned hot and dry, a condition that persisted for more than 3,000 years. The grassy prairies that dominated midwestern landscapes extended botanical fingers eastward into this encouraging environment, and the prairie plant community took hold in Pennsylvania's west about 2000 B.C. Then the restless forces of nature concocted a cooler, wetter climate, and most of the region became wooded. Hereabouts, however, the meager soil left by glaciers fended off the forests. Aided by fires and fauna that grazed on sapling trees, scraps of prairie held on. In 1902 Dr. Otto Emery Jennings, a renowned botanist from Pittsburgh's Carnegie Museum, first discovered this relict prairie. Today the **Jennings Environmental Education Center❖,** about five miles southeast of Slippery Rock on Route 528 east of I-79, instructs children and adults in indoor and outdoor classrooms. About 20 of the park's 300 acres are Pennsylvania prairie.

At first glance the shapes and shades of more than 50 plant species, stirred by warm summer breezes, sway and blur into a rainbow haze, like shifting clouds on the road to Oz. The superstar of this cast is the blazing star, also known as Kansas gayfeather. Hundreds of slender rods—drenched in clusters of fuzzy, rosy purple starbursts—rise four to six feet tall. Each flower is actually a group of blossoms—a composite—linked like webbing by tiny modified leaves called bracts. This outrageous, passionate purple spectacle usually erupts the first week of August; but if the weather changes, the show can debut anywhere from the last two weeks of July to the first half of August.

Although blazing stars are indeed the star plants, a galaxy of other wildflowers weave among them, waving languidly in polychromed glory on stalks two to ten feet tall. The supporting cast includes dusky rose–colored hollow joe-pye weed; orange coneflowers; yellow coreopsis; blue vervain and downy skullcap; purple swamp thistle, milk-

---

RIGHT: *Cattails edge a marsby pond in the Erie refuge, a major sanctuary for waterfowl. Although they resemble reeds, cattails are actually true flowers—with pollen-producing stamens and seed-bearing pistils.*

RIGHT: *Bright red ironweed and white Queen Anne's lace brighten a marsh in the Erie National Wildlife Refuge. Part of the parsley family, Queen Anne's lace has an edible root and is believed to be the ancestor of the cultivated carrot.*

wort, and ironweed; white meadowsweet; and pink steeple-bush, boneset, and wood candles. Although not all bloom at once, the prairie dazzles throughout mid- and late summer, when its wildflowers also attract hordes of butterflies and hummingbird moths.

Prairie notwithstanding, more than 400 plant species are Jennings residents, so blooming is nonstop from early spring well into autumn. Most of the preserve is forested, and clouds of woodland wildflowers color the shadowy glades in spring. Hundreds of warblers (35 species!) pass through in April and May. Also in May and occasionally as early as April, massasauga rattlesnakes begin to emerge from hibernation. These small, shy, secretive snakes have declined in numbers to become a "species of special concern" in the state. Despite their modest size and apparent timidity, they are potentially dangerous. Visitors should stay on the trails, and if they encounter a rattler, admire the elegant pattern of its skin from a distance.

The wildflower festival continues at **Wolf Creek Narrows Natural Area❖,** in a rural region outside Slippery Rock. Follow West Water Street northwest 1.7 miles from Route 258 in the center of town. A 1.5-mile trail leads upstream through open woodlands, following the creek as it flows between 50-foot-tall limestone bluffs that squeeze in on it, forcing the swift water into a narrower channel (the Narrows).

Initially the terrain is flat and treeless; in spring it suggests a skunk cabbage "farm" where clumps of buttercups and blue phlox poke up among the big green leaves. In summer Turk's cap lilies add flashes of hot orange. In the shady woods past a grove of tall sycamores, nature has landscaped a trillium garden, a vast carpet of multiple species of the tri-petaled beauties. The path heads up a slope where hepaticas—pink, blue, or white six-pointed stars—flower from rocky crevices. In the forest of beech and black cherry up top, another trillium garden forms a white cloud in early May. Between spring and summer more than 90 plants, including some rare ferns, can be found flourishing along Wolf Creek.

Follow a pair of wood ducks in this neighborhood, and they will probably lead the way to a wet, narrow valley ten miles east of Meadville on Route 198. The **Erie National Wildlife Refuge❖**, the only one of its kind in the state, has helped assure the continued existence of wood ducks. Early in the twentieth century the species appeared to be doomed by overhunting and habitat destruction. The creation of a federal chain of refuges—along with the nesting-box programs of state and federal wildlife agencies and stricter hunting regulations—restored wood duck populations to a more normal abundance. Today the male is America's handsomest duck, a flashy fellow distinguished by iridescent emerald-green head feathers flowing from the bill into a sleek swept-back crest.

Split into two units ten miles apart, the Erie refuge caters to the needs of waterfowl, shorebirds, waders, songbirds, and others with a

blend of marshes, swamps, creeks, man-made pools, and beaver ponds interspersed with grasslands, wooded slopes, wet meadows, and croplands growing grains that appeal to the birds. The refuge has attracted 236 species, both migrants and residents, and 112 of those have nested on the premises. Ducks are a site specialty; 12 species stop here, at least 8 of them in large numbers. On a busy day between March and early April, or September through November, the water-fowl tally can run to 2,500 ducks, plus 4,500 Canada geese.

Most people visit the refuge's **Sugar Lake Unit,** 5,206 acres next to the village of Guys Mills. The most popular trail is the Tsuga, which begins at the visitor center. It first passes sweeping fields of native grasses that provide dense, protective nest sites for ducks, mead-owlarks, bobolinks, red-winged blackbirds, and sparrows (13 species come here). Farther along, in a big man-made pond called an im-poundment, posts above the water hold nest boxes serving both wood ducks (the most prolific of local breeding ducks) and hooded mergansers. By late May or early June, duck parents are shepherding golden, downy offspring across the water.

Eventually the path becomes a long boardwalk across a pond. Rising from the murky surface is a spectral forest of pale gray, leafless trees and stumps killed by flooding when a beaver dam created the pond. The trees, called snags, are valuable for nesting and perching. Sudden flashes of electric blue streaking across the pond are probably tree swallows, which dart in and out of snag hollows to snare insects.

Less than 40 miles due north, birds congregate in even greater numbers and variety along the shore of Lake Erie at **Presque Isle State Park❖.** Only a short drive from downtown Erie (the state's third-largest city), Presque Isle appears on most lists of the top ten birding hot spots in North America. Its French name, which translates as "almost an is-land," is appropriate because the park occupies a peninsula—specifi-cally, a recurving sand spit—that from above resembles a giant lobster claw reaching out from shore for about seven miles. Only a few hun-dred yards wide at the entrance off Route 832, the low-lying spit

---

LEFT: *On Mill Road Beach in Presque Isle State Park, cottonwoods over-look the wind-ruffled waters of Lake Erie. Because its roots are so effi-cient at draining moisture from the soil, the cottonwood grows rapidly.*

Songbirds visiting Presque Isle include the American redstart (the female is shown above) and the veery (left), whose whistling notes often ring out in desolate swamplands.

spreads to a width of more than a mile at its center. Powerful currents and waves that could flatten a sizable building, both driven by prevailing westerly winds, stirred glacial sand deposits into this near-island roughly 600 to 1,000 years ago. As it juts into Lake Erie on a north-south axis, the peninsula is the last bit of land where northbound migrating birds can pause before a risky flight across the inland sea. Here location and projection concentrate tens of thousands of birds in a small area. Ornithologists call the phenomenon a funnel. When birds head south in autumn, it is the first landfall at the end of an exhausting overwater journey. As a result, the park has tallied 318 species, and most appear every year.

Migrants arrive in waves, beginning in late February with an advance guard of hawks; the raptors are most numerous in April. Nonresident waterfowl peak in March, and shorebirds start arriving in April. In May, birders toting binoculars and field guides descend like bees drawn to a cache of especially precious honey. Birds of prey have already peaked, but plenty still soar overhead. Shorebirds are at their height, skittering about beaches and muddy lagoon shores. Thirty-seven species have been recorded at Presque Isle, including large numbers from the plover and sandpiper families.

In the woods, tree limbs flush with new leaves vibrate with the agitated perpetual motion of male warblers in breeding plumage—countless variations on themes of blue, green, yellow, orange, and brown. Presque Isle tallies 33 warblers on a regular basis, plus a few others that drop in occasionally. Vireos, thrushes, tanagers, orioles, sparrows, flycatchers, wrens, swallows, finches, and more complete the Maytime songbird chorus. When a storm forces migrants out of the sky, birders can check off a hundred species or more in a couple of days.

176

Two perennial favorites of eastern wood-lands are the distinctive black-throated blue warbler (above) and the American goldfinch (left), a bird whose disposition is often said to match its cheery coloring.

During southbound migration, which begins in August, the sheer numbers of birds are less imposing, but the variety is just as great. In September, droves of monarch butterflies stop to feed on asters and other wildflowers as they steer toward winter sanctuaries to the south.

At Presque Isle, the botanically inclined can find more than 500 species of flowering plants and ferns. Something's blooming from early spring into early autumn. Among the rarest is the endangered Kalm, or brook, lobelia. In late July and August, its white-throated blue flowers dangle from tall, wispy stalks in wet areas.

Presque Isle is an ecological multiplex, containing within park borders the entire phenomenon of succession—from newly formed soil to climax forest. Ordinarily a trip of several hundred miles would be necessary to track the full progression. In a half-hour walk at this state park, however, visitors can follow 600 years of plant-life succession: sandbars and beaches with minimal vegetation; plains, dunes, and ridges with beach grasses, cottonwoods, willows, and various vines; dense shrubby thickets; mixed subclimax forest; and climax forest of red and black oaks, sugar maples, and hemlocks. Marshes, ponds, and lagoons separate the various stages. The whole sequence is condensed into a three-mile stretch, the only place in North America—possibly in the world—where this phenomenon occurs.

Cottonwoods, the most common trees in the park, stage quite a spectacle when they disperse their fluffy seeds, beginning the second week in June. To call the dispersal a summer snowstorm is not at all far-fetched. After two weeks, about four inches of cottonwood "snow" cover the ground. Another special event occurs more frequently. On clear summer days, when twilight approaches, the place to be is a point on the park's north shore near Budny Beach. Sky and lake flame

177

ABOVE: *A late fall sunset burnishes the landscape along Route 3005 in the Allegheny National Forest. Covering more than half a million acres, these woodlands are a mixture of hardwoods and conifers.*

in sunsets that aficionados rate the best in the Western Hemisphere, second only to Japan worldwide.

About 25 miles west of Erie near the Ohio border, the **David M. Roderick Wildlife Reserve**❖ hugs the shore of Lake Erie. (Head west on Route 20, and just west of a Y intersection with Route 5, turn north on Rudd Road. When Rudd dead-ends at Lake Shore Road, go west for nearly two miles to a parking area by a monument.) The 3,173 acres of uplands and wetlands—officially designated State Game Lands 314—once belonged to the United States Steel Corporation. On two occasions a major steel mill was planned for the property, but conservationists collaborated to keep it natural.

The reserve is elevated above the water on its most distinguishing physical feature, 30-to-40-foot-tall clay-and-silt bluffs. Colored yellow to gray, the steeply inclined cliffs undulate along the lakeshore. On warm days, bank swallows nesting in burrows in the upper edge of the bluffs execute remarkable acrobatics in pursuit of flying food. Although visitors can hike along the base of the bluffs, the trek is difficult, and the formations may be viewed with less effort from a windy, parklike overlook. In spring, this spot is ideal for watching hawks migrating north.

Birding is a year-round affair at Roderick, and migration seasons are particularly special. A single April day can turn up a hundred species. In early spring, male American woodcocks throw themselves into ath-

178

ABOVE: *In late November, Tioga State Forest takes on a wintry aspect. Small trees toppled in storms extend over Wilson Creek, which carries fallen leaves downstream as it flows between frost-covered banks.*

letic courtship displays in woodsy clearings along State Line Road. In the dim light of dawn and dusk, these chaps spin up into the sky, circle about, then flutter down in zigzag patterns like feathered tops as the females watch and judge.

THE NORTHERN PLATEAU AND THE GREAT UPLAND FORESTS

Of the forests that rule the landscape across Pennsylvania's northern tier, the most dramatic is sheltered in **Cook Forest State Park❖**, on Route 36 at Cooksburg. This 6,668-acre park is laced with some 30 miles of trails. The choicest, beginning behind the visitor center, leads to the **Cathedral Forest.** Rare and unusually large for the Northeast, this grove harbors virgin timber—white pines and hemlocks sprinkled with hardwoods, mostly beech. The forest probably began life late in the seventeenth century, and most of the trees are at least 200 years old, some more than 350. The term *cathedral,* occasionally used to describe forests that soar to a great height, is particularly appropriate at Cook Forest, where timber and terrain unite to create a Notre Dame of forests. The trail ascends a moderately steep incline that accentuates the thrust and scale of these lofty trees. Many pines rise above 200 feet and boast diameters of 4 feet.

The canopy at the peak of these colossal columns forms a near-

ABOVE: *A year before his death, Rubens Peale (1784–1865) painted* Two Grouse in an Underbrush *at Woodland Farm outside Philadelphia.*

solid ceiling, leaving the heavens barely visible and the forest floor dimly lit by slender shafts of light as if candles supplied the illumination. Heavily carpeted with needles and leaf litter, the floor muffles footsteps, and only occasional sounds—a fragment of birdsong or the nattering of a squirrel—penetrate the silence. The average church is noisy by comparison.

The **Allegheny National Forest**✤ on Route 62 is the biggest forest unit (about 512,000 acres) of any kind around these parts, even though it is broken up by numerous privately owned plots called inholdings. Although some areas are off limits to loggers, this working forest produces about 65 million board feet of timber, primarily hardwoods, each year. A short drive from the entrance, **Hearts Content Scenic Area**✤ may be explored on a generally level, 1.25-mile trail that winds through a 121-acre remnant of virgin timber at the headwaters of Tionesta Creek. In this old-growth mix of hemlock, white pine, beech, sugar maple, and black cherry, the hemlocks and pines rise tallest toward the clouds.

LEFT: *In Cook Forest State Park, white pines rise to majestic heights in Cathedral Forest. During storms, deer often huddle among the pines.*

181

ABOVE: *In Elk State Forest a bull elk displays his antlers; he sheds them after fall mating season when he no longer needs to battle rivals.*

Many of those are reputed to be more than 300 years old; some experts estimate 400. The canopy (nearly 200 feet at its maximum) is moderately open, allowing a surprising amount of sunlight to penetrate to the forest floor. As breezes riffle branches, light and shadow melt into ever-changing motley patterns.

Across the road from Hearts Content, a trailhead at the edge of a pine plantation is the first step into the **Hickory Creek Wilderness Area❖**, which contains substantial stands of tall timber but not virgin forest. It is second-growth hardwoods—notably beech, red oak, cherry, and hickory—plus occasional hemlocks. An 11.5-mile trail over rolling land loops through and around several stream valleys. The 8,750 acres of dense forest are dotted with bogs, meadows, beaver ponds, and creeks. Whenever sunlight penetrates, shrubs and wildflowers prosper.

A short distance east of the national forest, visitors can travel back some 250 years by having an elk encounter. We tend to picture elk, or wapiti (meaning white deer), as the Native Americans knew them, in settings similar to the meadows and mountain slopes of Yellowstone. Yet an eastern subspecies once flourished throughout Pennsylvania, New York, and New England. When Europeans toting rifles moved in, the elk was doomed, and by 1867, the eastern elk had been extirpated.

From 1913 to 1926, the state game commission tried to reintroduce Rocky Mountain elk at several locations, but the animals survived only in the north-central forest region. By the mid-1990s, the herd numbered about 200. They can be found at several locations in **Elk State Forest❖**

and adjacent state parks and game lands. Wild areas north of Benzette, on Route 555, tend to yield elk sightings. However, these unrestrained nomads are likely to roam from year to year, and the best tactic is to contact the District Forester Office in Emporium and ask directions.

Even from a distance, elk are impressive beasts. A mature male, or bull, weighs 600–1,000 pounds and measures 50–60 inches at the shoulder. The really big bruisers, rare imperial bulls, boast antler racks that stretch 5 to 6 feet in length and have 14 spikes, or points, (7 on each side). Royal bulls have 12 points. Cows, which have no antlers, weigh 400–600 pounds. The animals are more or less visible all year long, in family groups of cows, calves, and juvenile males. Mature bulls keep to themselves except for annual mating rites. In spring new calves—spotted like other deer fawns—nurse and follow their moms closely.

As a rule, elk behavior is not especially dramatic. The exception is the rut, or mating season, in September and October, when the bulls shatter the forest stillness with bugling, a bass bellow that rises to near-soprano register. They sustain that note as long as their breath holds out and then grunt repeatedly in an impressive if not exactly musical manner. Although bulls bugle at other times of year, in autumn they do it regularly, inviting females to an assignation while simultaneously challenging other bulls. The males lock antlers and spar for dominance and the right to mate with all the cows in the neighborhood. The pushing and shoving match continues until one warrior realizes he is outclassed and trots away to try again next year.

Bucktail State Park Natural Area❖, along Route 120 between Emporium and Lock Haven, isn't a park in the usual sense, but a 75-mile scenic drive. Often the road follows the west branch of Pennsylvania's largest river, the Susquehanna (although the river is not always visible). The route winds through a steeply sloping canyon forested with second-growth oaks and other hardwoods, hemlocks, and white and red pines. Near its eastern end are **Hyner Run** and **Hyner View State Parks❖.** The view over the Susquehanna, 1,300 feet below, and the wooded hills that caress its banks is a prizewinner, especially glorious the first two weeks of October, when leaf colors peak.

What better way is there to conclude a tour of the west than with a stop at the Grand Canyon? This site, however, is the Grand Canyon of Pennsylvania, **Pine Creek Gorge❖** in **Tioga State Forest.** At a maximum depth of 1,450 feet and a length of 47 miles, it is *slightly* smaller than that other Grand Canyon. The Pennsylvania gorge is a glacial gash produced by tons of meltwater from retreating ice and erosion by Pine Creek, which glacial debris dammed, reversing its flow from north- to southbound. Part of the gorge straddles two state parks, **Leonard Har-**

rison❖ on the eastern rim and **Colton Point❖** on the west. Here the ravine is only about 800 feet deep, but this section offers the best views.

Harrison, ten miles west of Wellsboro on Route 660, is the preferred starting point for most people. Its trails are less rigorous, and a good nature center provides an enlightening introduction to the gorge. To experience it from within, take the Turkey Path, a mile-long moderately steep, winding descent—sometimes along sheer cliffs—through beech and hemlock forest. Ferns and mosses decorate rocky ledges edging the path. About three-quarters of the way down, tough, resistant sandstone boulders turn a stream called Little Four-Mile Run into a series of cascading waterfalls.

ABOVE: *Sociable and frolicsome, the river otter is still holding its own despite the spreading ravages of water pollution.*

RIGHT: *In August, Pine Creek Gorge is shrouded in the white mist of dawn. To the left of the creek lies Leonard Harrison State Park, and to the right, Colton Point State Park.*

At the bottom is Pine Creek, a clean, clear tributary of the Susquehanna River. In summer its banks overflow with coneflowers, joe-pye weed, daisies, purple vervain, and other wildflowers. Birds in great variety are everywhere in the woods and along the stream. Bald eagles appear frequently. When the water level is high enough, usually April to early June and September through October, Pine Creek is navigable by canoes. In early October, the year's foliage begins its glorious exit, and bursts of orange, yellow, red, copper, and bronze flame like benign wildfires amid the green mantle over the gorge. By land or water, autumn is the super season at Pine Creek Gorge.

184

NEW JERSEY

PART THREE

N E W   J E R S E Y

According to an old joke, two individuals meet for the first time with this exchange: A: "Where are you from?" B: "New Jersey." A: "What exit?" The image of state as turnpike, however, is a false one—despite the statistics. New Jersey is the nation's fourth-smallest state, only 166 miles long with a land area of 7,836 square miles. It is home to nearly eight million people, ranking it eighth in population. In combination, those measurements make it the most densely populated of these United States, containing more than a thousand people per square mile.

Although it is indeed crowded, 40 percent of New Jersey's land is still forested. Its compact, superpopulated borders enclose 37 state parks, 11 state forests, 42 natural areas (some are wild spots within the parks and forests), and 65 wildlife management areas (WMAs alone comprise more than 200,000 acres). The state boasts more than 800 lakes and ponds and 127 miles of Atlantic shoreline, small segments of which remain relatively undeveloped and wild.

Wild and undeveloped it certainly was when Italian explorer Giovanni da Verrazano, the first European visitor, stopped by in 1524. After Henry Hudson claimed the area (including New York) for the Dutch in 1609, the colony of New Netherland was founded in 1623, and settlers began to alter the natural state. The English took control in 1664, splitting the colony into New Jersey and New York. One of the gentlemen granted title to the land was Sir George Carteret, a former governor of the Isle of Jersey in the English Channel, the source of the New Jersey name.

Industrial development got an early start thanks to the state's ample water supply and excellent natural harbors. The nineteenth-century construction of barge canals and railroads, followed by a sprawling web of highways in the twentieth, helped turn New Jersey into an industrial colossus dominated by chemicals, processed foods, pharmaceuticals, and machin-

---

PRECEDING PAGES: *Stratus clouds span the horizon at Cape May Point State Park as ocean breezes rustle the feathery phragmites on Bunker Pond.*

ery. Heavy industry proliferated almost exclusively in the north, although the sandy soil of South Jersey spawned a glassmaking industry. America's first glass factory opened in Salem County in 1735, and the industry thrived in the 1800s and early 1900s; a handful of factories still operate.

South Jersey is also responsible for the epithet Garden State. The 1920s through the 1940s were the heyday of New Jersey agriculture. Today farming has diminished somewhat, although Cumberland County remains a patchwork of large truck farms and fruit orchards. Specialty products such as Asian vegetables now find a ready market in New York and Philadelphia. Although not suited to conventional crops, the nearby Pine Barrens have been a rich source of berries. Cultivation of cranberries began in the early 1800s, and America's commercial blueberry industry was launched here early in the twentieth century.

All this development—industrial and agricultural—has been a mixed blessing. Thousands of wooded acres were stripped of vegetation, and the purity of many rivers, creeks, and wetlands was tainted, to put it mildly. Despite such troubles, natural sites are holding on.

The state has its share of scenic delights, but above all New Jersey is a birders' nirvana. Its location and peninsular landscape make it a crossroads of migration that hosts enormous numbers and varieties of both migrant and resident species. Although birding is usually associated with southern New Jersey, there is no shortage of sanctuaries in the north, some in heavily populated, highly unlikely spots. For example, an island in the Arthur Kill, a slender stream with a Dutch colonial name that separates a heavily industrialized section of New Jersey from New York's Staten Island, shelters large numbers of nesting egrets, herons, and ibises even though oil tankers and freighters cruise the waters nearby. The beleaguered island may not be the best of New Jersey nature, but it's an enormous improvement over past abuses.

Natural sites—both rough and pristine—have survived in New Jersey largely due to dedicated people in the state's parks, forestry, and wildlife management divisions. Equally important are several private conservation organizations such as the New Jersey chapter of the Nature Conservancy, which is responsible for many of the special places described in this book. The New Jersey Audubon Society, a homegrown outfit not related to National Audubon, maintains a splendid string of large and small preserves from north to south. Smaller and more specialized, the Pinelands Preservation Alliance labors to curb threats to a national natural treasure by educating the general public and elected officials. For anyone who is skeptical about nature in New Jersey, here's a suggestion: Get off the turnpike.

NORTHERN NEW JERSEY:
METROPOLIS TO MOUNTAINS

N orthern New Jersey is a study in contrasts—a landscape burdened by buildings and dense clusters of people that shifts abruptly to tree-covered mountains and clear, sparkling lakes. The upper two fifths of the state is neatly divided into three geologic provinces, approximately equal in size, that parallel one another along a northeast to southwest diagonal.

Easternmost, on the edge of New York City, some 1,500 square miles of Piedmont Lowland constitute about one fifth of the state. This region originally featured small rolling hills and was actually plateaulike in parts. The terrain's rolling aspect has largely been leveled and obscured because this area is the most crowded part of the most crowded state. A majority of New Jersey's biggest cities are here, plus many of modest size, one running smack into the next with no breathing space in between. These municipalities are linked by a dizzying network of highways and clouded by the fire and fumes belching from heavy concentrations of factories and refineries. Farther from that core, industrialization gives way to suburban sprawl, home to hundreds of thousands of commuters. Contained within this urban clutter, however, are a number of oases, soothing green shrines—some surprisingly large.

Farther west, yet less than an hour's drive from Manhattan, the population thins out in the Highlands, a quasi-wilderness of a thousand square miles that spills over into seven counties. Here broad,

LEFT: *Looking south toward the George Washington Bridge, the varied splendors of the New Jersey Palisades are manifest: terraced walls of igneous rock, luxuriant vegetation, and the broad, sparkling Hudson.*

flattened hills and mountains—nearly 1,000 to 1,500 feet above sea level—are cut by deep, narrow valleys that dip 400 to 600 feet below the crests of mountain ridges. The bedrock is some of America's most ancient, much of it nearly two billion years old. Greening the stone are vast, unbroken sweeps of timber where some trees, 300 to 400 years old and more, measure more than 15 feet around. Bobcat, black bears, and foxes prowl among them. About 260 bird species are residents or regular visitors; 140 of them nest here. Intact forest areas make the Highlands a special haven for migratory songbirds like warblers and vireos, whose populations elsewhere have declined in part because of forest fragmentation.

Rare plants thrive here, particularly in boggy sections. Streams of pure, untainted water race and sparkle through the forests, supporting healthy populations of trout and rare damselflies like the delicate lateral bluet. The Highlands are an enormous watershed, the source of drinking water for four million people, half the state population. They are in addition the scene of a classic conservation battle pitting environmentalists who want to preserve this treasure against developers who see only green dollar signs in the forests.

The westernmost section of northern New Jersey is the Valley and Ridge Province, part of a rippling series of parallel mountain ridges and valleys that follow the spine of the Appalachian Mountains from Canada's Saint Lawrence Valley to Georgia. Here the Kittatinny Mountains provide a sparsely populated, wild and woodsy sanctuary for abundant wildlife, especially bears and migrating hawks. This chapter begins at the Hudson River, travels west to several suburban islands of nature, then turns north into the Highlands and west to the Delaware. After following the river south, it edges eastward, concluding in the intellectual atmosphere of Princeton.

PIEDMONT: IN THE SHADOW OF GOTHAM

For 30 miles along the lower Hudson River—from Hoboken, New Jersey, north to Nyack, New York—a severe cliff wall rises 400 feet and more above the water. The dark rocks with their occasional flashes of red resemble a group of sharply angled vertical posts like those that once protected stockades. Hence their name, **The Palisades.** The supersolid rock, called diabase, began as molten magma that formed nearly

LEFT: *On a clear May morning, an aged willow displays new leaves as it enters another season beside a freshwater marsh in Troy Meadows.*

RIGHT: *Writing of the American bittern, Henry Thoreau noted that the marsh bird's cry can be compared to "a pump, or the chopping of wood in a frosty morning in some distant farm-yard."*

200 million years ago from deep below the earth's surface. The best closeup view is on the Palisades Interstate Parkway near State Line Lookout in **Palisades Interstate Park❖,** where two rugged trails lead down to the river shore and back up. The neck-craning view from below, imposing to say the least, is rendered the more dramatic by vegetation growing in the slope of talus, or shattered rocks that have tumbled to the base of the cliffs.

Although surrounded by horrendously busy major highways and somewhat fragmented, **Troy Meadows❖,** off Route 46 where I-280 crosses it near Parsippany, is one of the premier birding spots in North Jersey. The remains of an inland body of water created during the last ice age, Troy is one of the largest cattail freshwater marshes surviving in the state. Least and American bitterns and king, Virginia, and sora rail nest here. Although these reclusive birds hide in the dense, scruffy vegetation, their distinctive calls are often heard early in the day.

Other wildlife enriching the outing includes a colony of muskrat constructing hundreds of hummocky lodges from mud and cattails. Spotted and snapping turtles are possible sights, as are rare bog turtles, but they are hard to see because they are small and shy. Blue-spotted salamanders—usually found much farther north—appear here, but the chances of seeing one are slim.

April and May are peak months to visit. Early morning is best, just after daybreak for bitterns and rail. In spring the cattails are shorter, improving visibility, and the animals are more active—courting, nesting, and rearing young. Swamp sparrows and long-billed marsh wrens bounce on cattail spikes as they weave elaborate nests. Swooping in deep daredevil dives over the marsh, migrating common snipes mount a dazzling courtship display in April.

195

ABOVE: *Like all surface-feeding ducks, mallard rise directly from the water without any preliminary paddling to aid them in their takeoff.*

About 25 miles southwest of Manhattan's Times Square, the **Great Swamp National Wildlife Refuge** is a 7,200-acre miracle. It occupies the remnant of an ice age inland sea called Lake Passaic. During the nineteenth and early twentieth centuries, portions of the area were farmed, logged, drained, and otherwise abused. The gravest threat occurred in 1959, when the Port Authority of New York and New Jersey decided that the swamp would be a great place to build an airport. An aroused citizenry protested, lobbied, launched a public education program, raised money, and finally saved the swamp as a national wildlife refuge. Located just east of the town of Basking Ridge, the swamp still maintains a precarious existence.

A shallow bowl seven miles long and three miles wide, the refuge lies amid soft, rolling hills and low, narrow ridges. It encompasses a mix of hardwood swamp, marshes with open water, dense shrub thickets, upland forests, brooks, pasture, and cropland; the Passaic River forms its western border. Thanks to habitat diversity, nearly a thousand plant and animal species call the Great Swamp home for at least part of the year. Most abundant on the zoological side are birds,

RIGHT: *Elegant purple irises, squat green arrow arum, spiky bulrush sedge, and red maple seedlings populate a wetlands in the Great Swamp.*
OVERLEAF: *In La Plus Grande, a freshwater marsh in Lord Stirling Park, a boardwalk plunges through an array of burgeoning wetland plants.*

196

222 species, including warblers galore (especially in May). Mallard, black ducks, pintail, blue-winged and green-winged teal, shovelers, and wood ducks seek out the swamp, and many stay to nest. More than 500 pairs of wood ducks sometimes nest on the refuge, yielding thousands of downy ducklings. Ruffed grouse and woodcocks also nest here following their elaborate courtship rituals.

Of the 33 kinds of mammals, many are pocket-size creatures such as mice and voles. Red foxes are common, and white-tailed deer are abundant early and late in the day. Eight turtle species live in the swamp, along with 12 kinds of snakes (none venomous), a flock of frogs, and a splurge of salamanders. The refuge facilitates wildlife viewing with several miles of trails and boardwalks and two observation blinds.

Within the habitat are more than 250 plant species of both northern and southern botanical zones. Despite logging, some virgin timber survives, including impressive stands of beech, some with a girth of 14 feet. Growing atop little islandlike knolls, many of the beeches are estimated to be 300–500 years old.

Adjacent to the Great Swamp's western edge along the Passaic River, **Lord Stirling Park❖** is a bonus. About 425 acres of this 900-acre park are like an extension of the swamp; the rest is devoted to a stable and riding trails. Although the habitat, and the wildlife living in it, are almost identical to the Great Swamp's, the park merits a visit.

High points include La Plus Grande, a freshwater cattail marsh with great spreads of open water; a seasonally wet floodplain-woodland; both swamp woodland and dry forest; and abandoned farmlands reverting to forest. Visitors can navigate it all via 8.5 miles of flat, well-tended trails, 2 miles of boardwalk, numerous bridges, 2 observation blinds, and 2 observation towers.

THE HIGHLANDS

Among the reasons to venture into **Pyramid Mountain Natural Historical Area❖,** by the Boonton Reservoir on Route 511, are spectacular wildflower displays, lots of migratory birds, and uncluttered views

---

LEFT: *The pink flowers of Virginia rose alternate with narrow-leaved cattails in La Plus Grande marsh. The rose's fruit is a good source of vitamin C; the cattail's rootstock, shoots, and flowers are all edible.*

of Manhattan to the east. The most compelling reason is geologic whimsy in the form of glacial erratics.

Glaciers had an untidy habit of transporting boulders from their birthplaces and depositing them some distance away, often at locations where the erratics had no affinity to the bedrock beneath them. At Pyramid Mountain, **Tripod Rock** is an exceptional erratic, a 180-ton boulder balanced atop three much smaller rocks. Some people have speculated that members of the Lenni Lenape tribe did the balancing centuries ago, although how they accomplished such a feat without modern heavy construction equipment is a puzzle.

Two other boulders perched near Tripod Rock, however, may well have been put in place as part of a primitive astrological observatory. At the summer solstice, sunset appears directly between these rocks. Farther along the trail Bear Rock, one of the largest erratics in the state, is about ten times the size of Tripod Rock.

On Route 23 in the heart of the Jersey Highlands, **Wawayanda State Park❖** is the state's second largest. Encompassing 113,422 acres

ABOVE RIGHT: *Surprised during a nocturnal ramble, a raccoon seems more curious than alarmed. With deft paws and sharp teeth, these scavengers often hunt along streams, snaring frogs, fish, and turtles.*

along the New York border, Wawayanda is the premier officially protected site in the region and one of the few places in the Highlands where the billion-year-old granite that forms the bedrock of the region is exposed to view. The park's name comes from a Lenni Lenape word meaning "water on the mountain," a reference to 265-acre Wawayanda Lake. Much of the land was heavily logged in the 1940s, and a major iron forge was located here in the mid-1800s. Nevertheless, in its dense tree canopies that cast most trails into shadows, its array of pristine wetlands, and its impenetrable rhododendron "jungles," Wawayanda captures the feeling and quality of wilderness today.

Nearly a third of the park has been set aside in natural areas. For example, **Bearfort Mountain Natural Area**❖ is a 1,325-acre mosaic of hardwood swamp forest, an emergent marsh, and several forest communities in which specific tree mixes dominate: oak-hardwood, hemlock–mixed hardwood, and chestnut oak. Amid the deciduous woodlands, visitors can see a variety of large birds such as broadwinged hawks, great horned and screech owls, ruffed grouse, black-billed and yellow-billed cuckoos, and pileated woodpeckers. Like the rest of the Highland region, Wawayanda is an important migratory stopover for tiny songbirds known as Neotropical migrants, such as warblers and vireos.

The **Hemlock Ravine Natural Area❖,** a patchwork of hardwood species and hemlocks on 402 acres, is a sanctuary for such endangered plants as Dewey's sedge, witch hobble, and white-grained mountain rice grass. The **Wawayanda Swamp Natural Area❖** supports groves of northern white cedar, a species at the southern tip of its range here and rarely seen in New Jersey. Atlantic white cedar, usually found at lower elevations near seacoasts and thus common in South Jersey, also thrives here slightly out of its element, rising in clumps from sphagnum-moss-draped hummocks. This 2,164-acre area also contains a northern glacial bog that blends mixed oak–hardwood and hemlock forests. Although bears and bobcat leave their prints in this country, they are seldom seen during daylight hours.

The **Wallkill River National Wildlife Refuge❖,** on Route 284 northeast of Sussex, is one of America's newest sanctuaries. The Appalachian Trail passes through the northernmost section of the refuge, making it the only refuge in the country that hosts the Appalachian Trail. Slated to cover 7,500 acres on the Wallkill River floodplain, the refuge is at the western edge of the Highlands. About 4,200 acres are wetlands—including palustrine (wet) forest, emergent marsh, wet meadows, shrubby marsh, and ponds—and another 3,300 are upland forest. The site straddles two major migration corridors for waterfowl traveling along the Atlantic Coast to eastern Canada: the Delaware and Hudson rivers. The Wallkill River's bottomlands are one of the very few large, high-quality waterfowl habitats left in the state. Ducks and geese by the thousands nest here or stop to feed and rest during migration. The refuge is especially important to black ducks, wood ducks, mallard, American woodcocks, and great blue herons; it contains one of the largest heron colonies in the state.

Wallkill is also a haven for dwindling grassland birds, and in spring

RIGHT: *In June, the pink-and-white flowers of crown vetch enliven a swamp near Wawayanda. Because vetch roots contain nitrogen-fixing bacteria, they are often planted to increase soil fertility.*

ABOVE: *The East's largest wading bird, the great blue heron has a wingspan equal to an eagle's, and its powerful neck and serrated bill are devastatingly efficient.*

RIGHT: *In June, the Wallkill River is awash in greenery: duckweed on the water, arrow arum at water's edge, maples on the banks.*

bobolinks and grasshopper and savannah sparrows cheep and chip, bubble and buzz as they cling to tall emerging grasses stirred by erratic breezes. Neotropical migrant songbirds—warblers, vireos, orioles, and more—flock to refuge uplands. Large residents on the premises include black bears, bobcat, coyotes, river otters, mink, and red and gray foxes.

THE KITTATINNY RIDGE AND THE DELAWARE RIVER

Tucked into New Jersey's northwest corner on Route 23 about 12 miles northwest of Sussex, **High Point State Park❖** claims the state's ultimate escalation: 1,803 feet. Atop the peak is a 220-foot memorial obelisk. When it's open, visitors can climb to the top for a panoramic view of the Delaware Water Gap and Pocono Mountains to the west and the Wallkill River valley and Catskill Mountains to the east and north.

Surrounding the monument is the **Dryden-Kuser Natural Area❖**, occupying some 1,451 of the park's 14,000-plus acres. A combination of footpath and boardwalk follows the site's perimeter and cuts through its center. The leaf-carpeted path edges the cedar swamp, a

boggy tangle of tall, thick trees and weedy saplings; gnarly uprooted trunks draped with mosses and lichens, poking from patches of soupy, perfectly placid water; mats of sphagnum moss; fallen logs; stumps; and ferns, ferns, ferns. Rhododendrons rampage through the understory, virtually walling off entire sections. In less crowded spots highbush blueberries flash wine-red leaves in the fall, and mountain holly, a very rare shrub in New Jersey, makes an appearance.

Shafts of dappled light filter down through the canopy, illuminating the dominant, virtually virgin trees: hemlocks, white pines, black spruces, and southern white cedars, unusual at this high an altitude. Bereft of lower branches, the cedar trunks are wrapped in wrinkled reddish bark; lichens filling vertical indentations resemble tarnished copper against the brick red bark. In their upper reaches, the branches weave a twisted path, ending in knots of needles. Stillness cloaks the scene except for avian visitors—cedar waxwings, chickadees, blue jays, white-breasted nuthatches, winter wrens, and other feathered creatures bouncing around the branches.

207

Tillman Ravine in **Stokes State Forest❖** (adjacent to the south end of High Point) would probably win an award in a contest for the prettiest walk in New Jersey. (It's also a great place to observe mushrooms in the fall.) Almost anyone can do this easy walk in less than an hour. The trail follows Tillman Brook as it meanders through the ravine, a remnant of the last glacial era. Ferns drape across the rocky banks splotched with lichens as water bubbles and splashes around boulders. Occasionally the stream pours over a small precipice to become a little waterfall. At some spots, the water has agitated sand and gravel and scoured potholes in the bedrock, most notably the Teacup, a deep rounded bowl about six feet in diameter near the bottom of the gorge.

In the silence of the ravine, the brook percolates with restraint, then generates a surprisingly loud roar for a relatively small stream. Suddenly it rides down a flume—sliding, dropping, splashing crazily over a grand waterslide. The water splits around a moss-mottled boulder, leaps over a ledge like a proper waterfall, reunites to pool and spin in a basin, then splits again into main and tributary flows. Shifting direction, it repeatedly splits and spins, constantly redefining itself, oblivious to woodland debris trying to block its path.

Extravagantly green, the forest's tall hemlocks form a dense canopy, shading the area deeply. Stream and shade have combined to produce a cool microclimate more typical of latitudes much farther north. Big boulders and fallen trees along the stream are upholstered with velvety deep-green moss. Where hemlocks have fallen and opened up the canopy, hardwoods have sprung up, lending contrast, especially in autumn when seasonal colors explode. Where it can break through, sunlight floods the brook, exposing kaleidoscopic patterns amid the whirling water. All along the ravine walls, rhododendrons dominate the understory and in July provide an extravagant floral display. From April through July, wildflowers bloom in shades from subtle to brilliant. Because of the ravine's habitat and pocket of cool climate, several warbler and other songbird species that would not normally nest this far south choose to travel no farther than Tillman. In this shaded,

---

LEFT: *Drooping boughs of towering hemlocks filter the sunlight in Tillman Ravine, where a cool, damp climate fosters the growth of mosses and mushrooms. Deer feed on needles that carpet the forest floor.*

secluded haven, made musical by the melodies of rushing water and birdsong, New York City seems a world away, even though it's only about two hours' drive.

Spanning both sides of the middle Delaware River for 40 miles, the **Delaware Water Gap National Recreation Area❖** occupies 70,000

acres of New Jersey and Pennsylvania along the riverbanks. Except for a small southern portion, the park extends north of I-80 almost to the intersection of New Jersey, Pennsylvania, and New York. The river cuts through the Kittatinny Mountains, twisting into a tight S-shaped bend. River, mountains, and forest collaborate in a scenic elegance that has drawn hordes of vacationers since early in the nineteenth century.

Above: *Once seen as a sly villain, the red fox is really just a shy omnivore; its bushy tail covers its tracks in the snow.*
Right: *At the Delaware Water Gap, Buttermilk Falls gently descends over sandstone ledges covered with moss and lichen.*

Many people insist that the only way to appreciate the park is from the river—via canoe, raft, or inner tube. On New Jersey turf, visitors can also explore the river on Old Mine Road, which runs the entire length of the park from the Kittatinny Point Visitor Center just off I-80 to the intersection of Route 6 (outside the park). Historians believe that the road is one of the oldest highways of any significant length in North America. Traveling through forest much of the time, it offers the best way to get close to the river without a boat. Other traffic is rare, and the drive is like following a backcountry road in the 1930s and 1940s. Here and there, small openings in the forest permit views of the river. Farther north are spots where visitors can pull off to picnic or just admire the riverscape. Deep blue water, sometimes tinted brown, sweeps between tree-filled shores, occasionally navigating around wooded islands. In October, a cornucopia of color spills across the riverbanks and paints the water with fiery reflections.

Eventually the road veers away from the river. Turn off at Walpack (a

ABOVE: *In early summer, prickly pear cacti bloom at Milford Bluffs. Although it lacks the spines of its western cousins, the eastern prickly pear has bristles (known as glochids) equipped with pointed barbs.*

village that now houses park personnel) to find an old cemetery. Where the graves end, a right turn onto a gravel (then dirt) road leads, after two miles, to **Buttermilk Falls,** one of New Jersey's tallest. A mountain drainage, the slender stream slips nearly a hundred feet through a deeply shadowed crevice on the north slope of Kittatinny Ridge. As it flows through a channel of rust-colored sandstone, the water bounces over a series of terraces, slides along rock faces, and widens into pools as it nears bottom. At times it appears to be a series of separate streams. The tumble over multiple rocks aerates the clear water, turning it so white that it looks for all the world like spilling buttermilk.

Nearby is one of the park's finest vistas, **Raccoon Ridge.** (Follow the Kaiser Road Trail from the Copper Mine parking area off Old Mine Road to the Appalachian Trail, 25 miles of which run along the park's eastern edge. Turn south until the path reaches a bald spot, opening to a view of river and valley 1,200 feet below.) The colors are spectacular in autumn, and this north-facing ridge is supreme for observing birds of prey migrating south over the Kittatinny Mountains. The spectacle begins in late August and continues into December, when bald and golden eagles soar past. Viewing is best on clear, brisk, windy days.

Farther south along the Delaware River awaits a scene seemingly magically transported from Arizona and installed outside the little town of Milford. Heading toward the river on Bridge Street, turn north just before the bridge and follow the road about half a mile out of town. Looming above are the **Milford Bluffs**—sheer red-shale cliffs rising vertically from the road's edge and covered with more than a thousand prickly pear cacti (*Opuntia*). For about two weeks in mid-June, the dark green barbed and flattened pads of cacti deck the cliffs with vivid lemon yellow blossoms. Highlighted by the brick red shale, the prickly pears make an exceptional rock garden, the likes of which won't be found elsewhere in the state or in many other states. An array of rare wildflowers that thrive on dry sites augment the succulent display. Following their bloom, the cacti produce the oblong purplish-pink "pears" for which they are named. Even when the pricklies are not blooming or fruiting, the clusters of spiny plants on these red cliffs are an exceptional sight.

Ken Lockwood Gorge Wildlife Management Area❖—on Raritan River Road off Route 513, east of Voorhees State Park—bears a strong resemblance to Tillman Ravine (see pages 208–9). The focus of the 260-acre refuge is the south branch of the Raritan River, more of a wild stream than Tillman Brook. Between banks shaded by tall hemlocks and hardwoods, the Raritan thunders through the ravine at a volume that seems out of proportion to the river's size. Near the beginning of the trail, the Raritan collides with an island and forks into dual channels, equally energetic. The island is top-heavy with hemlocks, and the area around it tends to be cool even on hot days. The twin streams reconnect at island's end and rush on, tearing around blotchy boulder behemoths. The Raritan is more rapids than babbling brook, and waterfalls are uncommon. Occasionally, swirling pools calm the river's rush, then it charges forward again. A perfect setting for trout (brook, brown, and rainbow), the Raritan is extremely popular with anglers and on spring and summer weekends the gorge can be crowded.

About half a mile from the ivy-clad halls of Princeton University is a place that attracts flocks of birds and birders every spring. Actually two places, adjacent to each other, the **Charles H. Rogers Wildlife Refuge❖** and the **Institute Woods❖** are off Alexander Street, one of the town's main thoroughfares. Together the sanctuaries total nearly 550

213

LEFT: *Once nearly extinct, the chestnut-sided warbler is now heard throughout the East in spring and summer; it winters in Central America.*

RIGHT: *On a July evening, a determined fly fisher goes in pursuit of an elusive trout in the swift current of the Raritan River's southern branch.*

acres, a felicitous blend of deciduous woodlands, open marsh, and riparian forest. About 5:30 A.M. in early to mid-May, the Rogers refuge is engulfed by an unceasing chorus of birdsong, a mingling of melodies that birders try desperately to sort out and track to specific locations.

Near the parking area, an observation platform affords a view of the marsh. Clinging to tall reeds, red-winged blackbirds challenge each other with gurgling, buzzing trills. Tree swallows dart in and out of houses erected on poles in the water to encourage nesting. Gleaning upper tree branches for caterpillars, northern orioles form orange sunbursts amid emerging leaves. Wood ducks pad about the wetland or along branches of bordering trees, where they nest in hollows. Canada geese drift among the reeds, occasionally exploding into brief, noisy territorial disputes.

Woodland paths, including one following Stony Brook, are abloom with dogwoods, spring beauties, and violets. Members of the human population stroll about with heads tilted back and binoculars clamped to eyeballs, surveying tangles of willows, honeysuckle bushes, maples, oaks, and various vines. Visitors would be hard-pressed not to find such birds as rose-breasted grosbeak males—feathered firecrackers with a vibrant red patch on their white upper breast that sing as if to imitate a robin—or yellow-billed and black-billed cuckoos, foot-long birds with curving beaks and long tails.

At the Institute Woods, the path marches between forest and open fields, then becomes totally wrapped in woods. In May, warblers are as thick as gnats—yellow, magnolia, Kentucky, blue-winged, and sometimes, along Stony Brook, the elusive prothonotary. On a fairly decent day, birders commonly log 25 warbler species, and 30 is not unknown. Many call it the best spot in the state for migrating songbirds.

SOUTHERN NEW JERSEY
BIRDS, BOGS, BARRENS, AND BEACHES

Anyone flying south over New Jersey could not help notic-
ing an abrupt transition from the hills of the north to the
pancake flatness of the south. A few miles north of the
deep notch that the Delaware River has carved in the
state's western edge, an invisible boundary angles northeastward from
Trenton to New Brunswick and then to Perth Amboy on the coast,
more or less following the paths of Route 1 and Amtrak's northeastern
corridor rail line. This diagonal is known as the fall line, referring to a
series of falls and rapids. The term originated during the colonial era,
when the landscape was less cluttered and the falls easier to see.

The roughly 4,500 square miles of South Jersey—about three fifths
of the state—occupy the coastal plain, a geologic province that traces
the Atlantic shore from Cape Cod to Georgia. More than half the terrain is lower than 100 feet in elevation, and its highest point does not
reach 400 feet. The soil here is predominantly sand, sometimes blended with silt and various clays. To most of the state's residents, South
Jersey means the Shore, a long series of beaches and barrier islands
largely devoted to family resort communities. A few choice wetlands,
fortunately left intact, now comprise some of the Northeast's finest nature refuges. On the western side of the Cape May peninsula, the
shores of Delaware Bay remain primarily a chain of wetlands, most of

LEFT: *The Cape May Lighthouse rises above a reed-filled marsh at Cape*
May Point State Park. Jutting out from the coast, Cape May is a choice
stopover point on the Atlantic Flyway, attracting both birds and birders.

them protected areas designated to preserve flora and fauna.

Between the Delaware River and the Atlantic Ocean stretch some 2,000 square miles called the Pine Barrens or Pinelands, an internationally recognized wetland wilderness that is the point of origin for two national wild and scenic rivers and home to an abundance of rare plants and animals. Because the South Jersey climate is much milder and rainier than North Jersey's, 116 plants normally found only in southern states flourish here, growing no farther north than Burlington County, where most of the Pinelands lie.

Cape May, the southern tip of this northern state, is actually below the Mason-Dixon line, farther south than Baltimore. Although it can be chilly in January, the weather is relatively benign. Famous since the nineteenth century as a picturesque resort community, Cape May has become *the* American mecca for birders thanks to the year-round presence of millions of birds, both residents and migrants.

Beginning its South Jersey tour in the west of the state at Trenton, this chapter travels northeast to Sandy Hook. It then proceeds south along the Atlantic Ocean, with occasional jogs inland, concluding at land's end, Cape May.

INTERIOR WETLANDS TO THE ATLANTIC COAST

Although many New Jerseyans consider Trenton, the state capital, a political swamp, a more appealing and productive wetland lies on the city's southern outskirts. The **Hamilton/Trenton Marsh❖** is a wetland complex of tidal and nontidal marshes, ponds bedecked with dense vegetation, shrubby islands, meandering streams, wet forest swamps, and pockets of upland second-growth forest. Its 1,250 acres harbor more than 700 plant species and 230 types of birds. Its existence is something of a miracle because an interchange connecting three highways was constructed near the heart of the wetlands in the 1990s.

The most accessible section is in **Roebling Memorial Park❖**, 200 acres of tidal marsh, freshwater ponds, and woodlands on Sewell Avenue off Route 206 in Hamilton. A causeway follows the bank of Spring Lake, whose surface resembles a vast plain of giant leaves, most shaped like the spades on a deck of cards: water lilies, arrow arum, arrowhead, and pickerelweed. In summer, spikes of violet blue pickerelweed blossoms bristle with nectar-loving butterflies.

10   0   10 Miles

10   0   10 Kilometers

NEW

YORK

PENNSYLVANIA

DELAWARE

Delaware River

206

95

Sandy Hook Bay

GATEWAY NAT
RECREATION AREA

36

9

Highlands

HUBER
WOODS

ROEBLING
MEMORIAL PARK

33

TRENTON

295

HAMILTON-
TRENTON
MARSH

Hightstown

ASSUNPINK
WMA

276

95

Hamilton

Bordentown

GARDEN STATE PKWY

195

Camden

LEBANON
STATE
FOREST

GREENWOOD
FOREST
WMA /
WEBBS MILL
BOG

Toms
River

TURNPIKE

206

73

Berlin

OSWEGO RIVER NATURAL AREA

Atsion

WHARTON
STATE FOR

72

WEST PINE
PLAINS
NATURAL
AREA

ISLAND BEACH
STATE PARK

9

NEW JERSEY

55

Mullica R

Long
Beach
Island

Pleasant
Mills

Tuckerton

*Little Egg
Harbor*

GREAT EGG HARBOR WILD & SCENIC RIVER

Penny Pot

Oceanville

Great Bay

GREAT BAY BOULEVARD
WILDLIFE MANAGEMENT AREA

MAURICE WILD & SCENIC RIVER

Weymouth

Great Egg Harbor River

EDWIN B. FORSYTHE
NATIONAL WILDLIFE REFUGE

9

Millville

55

BELLEPLAIN
STATE FOREST

Atlantic
City

Great Egg Harbor

Mauricetown

9

DENNIS CREEK
WILDLIFE
MANAGEMENT AREA

REED'S BEACH

47

Stone
Harbor

Hereford Inlet

HIGBEE BEACH WMA

North Wildwood

CAPE MAY
BIRD OBSERVATORY

Cape May

Delaware Bay

CAPE MAY
POINT SP

CAPE MAY MIGRATORY
BIRD REFUGE

Pied-billed grebes nest around the lake in spring, along with least and American bitterns and a couple of rail species, all vocal but usually invisible. Green herons are more commonly seen, and chipper little marsh wrens often perch atop cattails. In the earth at the edge of the path, red-bellied turtles, a southern species, excavate shallow nests.

A rather different perspective awaits in the marsh's **Bordentown Bluffs** section, on Glen Road off Route 206 in Bordentown. In this area, part of an estate that once belonged to Joseph Bonaparte, brother of Napoleon, tall bluffs loom over the swift mud-colored creek. Lining its banks are sweeping patches of wild rice eight to ten feet tall and in late summer topped with sprays of seeds that birds love. Scattered along the banks are the bright yellow flowers of fringed loosestrife, and in late summer a rarer yellow beauty, the bur marigold, takes over. Great stands of cattails and reeds rise from the water. The forest here is populated with stands of hemlock and black birch and an understory of rhododendrons and mountain laurel.

Midway between the Delaware River and the Atlantic Coast, **Assunpink Wildlife Management Area❖** is a 5,400-acre refuge south of Hightstown. (For directions contact the office in Robbinsville.) At this open oasis amid industrial development and agriculture, varied habitats (man-made lakes, fields, hedgerows, lowland deciduous forest, upland woods, and marsh) lure about 250 species of birds each year. The lake is an excellent locale to view waterfowl during spring and fall migrations. More ring-necked ducks come here than to any other location in the state, and as many as 2,300 common mergansers also appear. Pied-billed grebes nest here, and both horned and red-necked grebes are regular visitors. In spring and fall, thousands of swallows dart over the lake hawking insects. Although most are tree swallows, greenish blue blurs in the air, hundreds of purple martins and bank, barn, and rough-winged swallows also visit.

One of four units in the **Gateway National Recreation Area, Sandy Hook❖** is a 6.5-mile sand spit poking north into the Atlantic Ocean. The 160-acre park is off Route 36 in Highlands. Along the Old

LEFT: *The rose-tinted glow of a June sunset is mirrored in the still waters of Assunpink Lake. In the foreground, milkweed stalks tower over the blunt green leaves of arrow arum and dense panic grass.*

221

LEFT: *Because of its reddish breast patch in spring and summer, the red knot is also known as the robin snipe. In fall, the front of this shorebird turns nearly white.*
RIGHT: *On a clear September morning, New York harbor, Manhattan skyscrapers (center), the Brooklyn shoreline (right), and the Verrazano-Narrows Bridge (left) are clearly visible from Sandy Hook.*

Dune Trail, clumps of prickly pear cactus drape across sandy pillows. Nearby are salt marshes, three freshwater ponds, and a variety of forests, such as the national natural landmark forest of American holly, which is sprinkled with scattered shadbush and black cherry trees. The holly trees, many more than 150 years old, thrive in the sand and salt air, sending roots down several feet to find water. Their shiny, spiky, leathery leaves prevent them from losing the precious moisture. By late summer and early fall, they are loaded with clusters of crimson berries, a feast for countless birds.

One of the best birding spots on the east coast, Sandy Hook from March 15 through May 15 is one of the few really great places to see hawks during spring migration. April is the peak, although great horned owls and ospreys stay around longer to breed in the woodsy, marshy parts of Sandy Hook. A great variety of terns, gulls, and shorebirds stop on the beaches; grassy fields lure sparrows, meadowlarks, and bobolinks; and wooded areas are flooded with warblers, vireos, flycatchers, thrushes, and songbird migrants in April, May, and August through October.

A bit inland from Sandy Hook, on the peninsula that separates Sandy Hook Bay and the Navesink River, lies a stately 255-acre coastal-plain forest. Although a variety of mixed hardwoods thrive here, **Huber Woods Park and Environmental Center❖** is dominated by five species of oak, which have grown very large and are entwined with climbing vines. The rich understory is thick with shrubs that produce banner crops of berries enjoyed by numerous forest birds, and the forest floor stages a glorious display of wildflowers in the spring.

Stretching along the state's Atlantic coast is a chain of barrier islands, most of them packed with vacation homes. **Island Beach State Park❖,** east of Toms River, is a rare exception, a ten-mile strip that re-

ABOVE: *Black-eyed Susans enliven a summer meadow in Huber Woods. The flower heads are actually composites—disk flowers form the brown cones of the central "eye," and buttery ray flowers grow underneath.*

mains a pristine barrier beach. The central portion of the park's 3,001 acres is given over to recreation, and summer weekends can log 10,000 to 15,000 visitors per day. The northern and southern thirds of the park, however, are rigidly restricted to plants and animals, but may be visited on scheduled naturalist-led tours. Within the fragile natural areas are coastal dune grasslands, shrubby thickets (lots of berry bushes), woodlands, freshwater bogs, and salt marshes.

At the ocean, low dunes ripple like sandy waves toward the water, anchored by clumps of beach grass whose roots spread out to stabilize the sand. A few other salt-tolerant plants help—such as seaside goldenrod, which sports fleshy leaves and curving yellow flower plumes atop eight-foot stalks. In early summer the low back dunes glow golden as carpets of tiny yellow *Hudsonia* flowers open. Also called false heather or beach heath, this matted evergreen thrives in the extremely dry environment. Tiny pale purple accents are blooming sea rockets. Bushy, low-growing beach plums straggle over the sand, producing little white flowers from April to June. In September and October the beach plums ripen. Taller back dunes shield thickets of American holly, shadbush, bayberry, blueberry, and black cherry.

Because of its location on the Atlantic Flyway and its habitat diversity, Island Beach is also a superb birding spot: 240 species have been

ABOVE: *The Nature Loop Trail in Huber Woods winds through lush summer vegetation. Tall woodland, or Dryopteris, ferns cluster in the foreground; beyond, a red maple is host to luxuriant climbing grapevines.*

recorded. Countless songbirds pause here during migration, and gulls, terns, and shorebirds frequent the park most of the time, many nesting here. The barrier island draws quite a crowd of sparrows, many of them species seldom seen: lark, clay-colored, vesper, Lincoln's, white-crowned, and in winter, the Ipswich race of the savannah sparrow.

THE PINELANDS

Sprawling over nearly a quarter of the state less than a hundred miles from New York City and Philadelphia is a sparsely populated wilderness called the **Pine Barrens❖.** This rare blend of wetlands and dry, sandy uplands occupies 1.1 million acres, atop a remarkable and precious resource, the Cohansey-Kirkwood aquifer, an underground reservoir holding 17 trillion gallons of water. The aquifer may be invisible, but the surface offers lots to see. In the flat, wooded Pine Barrens, the last vast forested area on the mid-Atlantic coast, more than 800 plant species have been identified. Along with 23 types of orchids, the inventory includes 109 southern species that hit the northern end of their ranges in the Barrens. Another 14 species normally occur much farther north and reach their southern limit here.

Wildlife also exhibits an end-of-the-range tendency, but includes far fewer species, all southerners. The most exceptional group is herpeto-

225

logical: 15 frogs and toads, 11 salamanders, 19 snakes, 3 lizards, and 12 turtles. A principal attraction is the endangered Pine Barrens tree frog, a chunky little emerald-green beast with a broad band of purple edged by a pencil-thin white border that lives only here and at a handful of isolated southern locations. Although colorful, the tree frog is not easily seen because it is only 1.5 inches long and active at night. Visitors can sometimes see one or at the very least, they can hear the nasal *quonk! quonk!* of the lust-crazed males that begins around dusk during the mid-May-to-mid-June mating season. Marginally more musical is the dapper yellow-brown carpenter frog. A carpenter colony serenade sounds as if a large crew were constructing a house and hammering nails in rapid succession. Often the carpenters share habitat with the tree frogs.

ABOVE: *The diminutive nocturnal Pine Barrens tree frog seldom exceeds two inches in length and is rarely observed.*

LEFT: *Batonia Trail crosses a heavily wooded swamp in Lebanon State Forest, zigzagging past red maples, black gums, and pitch pines.*

Despite the land's obvious botanical extravagance, eighteenth-century European settlers found its sandy, acidic soil too infertile for standard agricultural crops and labeled the area the Pine Barrens. Over the decades, it has also come to be known as the Pinelands. In 1983, UNESCO's Man and the Biosphere Program recognized the New Jersey Pine Barrens as one of the world's outstanding natural areas, a place meriting serious protection. Providing that protection since 1978 is the **Pinelands National Reserve,** the only such reserve in the United States. Under the jurisdiction of the National Park Service, the reserve is managed by a state commission.

To explore the Pinelands, a good starting point is the 32,000-acre **Lebanon State Forest❖** on Route 72, where more than 200 miles of roads and trails enable visitors to venture into wild and semiwild regions. In the **Cedar Swamp Natural Area❖** near forest headquarters, Atlantic white cedars, tall, majestic dark-green trees, cluster in dense stands along swamp water. Slender and conical, the cedars grow on spongy hummocks with sphagnum moss matted around their buttress roots; as many as 4,000 trees may occupy a single acre. Because the

LEFT: *The fruits of a high-bush blueberry shrub ripen in Lebanon State Forest. Mammals and birds not only feed on the plant's tasty dark-blue berries but also consume its soft twigs and glossy green leaves.*
RIGHT: *Thick grasses and still waters pervade a cranberry bog in Lebanon State Forest. Cranberries remain on plants all winter, brightening barren landscapes.*

cedars are so thick, their canopy creates a very dark forest, hospitable only to shade-loving plants such as several rare orchids and insectivorous plants such as sundews and pitcher plants. In the forest of pitch pines ringing the swamp, dry, sunny spots harbor a very different array of plants. Pyxie moss (not a moss at all) trails its five-petaled white blossoms across sandy spots in early spring. Another scraggly shrub, sand myrtle, produces clusters of tiny pink-to-white flowers from late April into early June. This raw, sandy habitat turns bright yellow in late May, when a shrub called *Hudsonia,* or beach heath, blooms in hundreds of minuscule flowers. About the same time, turkey beard, a grasslike plant of the pitch pine environment, produces dense clusters of tiny feathery white flowers atop a spindly stalk.

Webbs Mill Bog, on the east side of Route 539 in the **Greenwood Forest Wildlife Management Area❖,** concentrates an exceptional profusion of flora within a compact area. The landscape is dominated by hummocks of sphagnum moss and evergreen leatherleaf growing over a sand foundation. Here visitors with a botanical bent can see curly grass fern, whose twisty, grasslike stems end in fronds resembling a pair of toothy tongs. Only five inches tops and easily overlooked, this endangered fern is usually found in the Maritime Provinces of Canada. The waters of Webbs Mill are a menace to invertebrates because they teem with carnivorous pitcher plants, three kinds of sundews ready to clamp gummy pads on unsuspecting bugs, and six species of bladderworts, which trap tiny aquatic creatures in numerous little bladders attached to their underwater leaves.

ABOVE: *The swamp pink, an arethusa orchid, often grows in sphagnum bogs. The plant's erect sepals and drooping lip have earned it the nickname dragon's mouth.*

RIGHT: *After a wildfire in Greenwood Forest WMA, shrubs of the heath family sprout from rhizomes, and new growth appears on the charred pitch pines.*

From spring into fall, the bog dazzles with colors that change with the calendar. Beginning in mid-April, the globelike blossoms of swamp pinks adorn green spikes emerging from clusters of big fleshy, pointy leaves. Mid-May to mid-June brings the dramatic arethusa orchid, a complex magenta blossom with a drooping yellow tongue flecked with purple. Appearing at the same time are the vivid yellow starlike flowers of bog asphodel. From early June to early July the pure white blossoms of clammy azalea brighten the bog, and in mid-August bog aster produces daisylike blossoms varying from violet to purple. Nearly all these plants are classified as threatened or endangered. Webbs Mills is also a splendid place to seek the Pinelands' colorful and varied reptiles and amphibians.

The **West Pine Plains Natural Area❖,** on Route 72 two miles west of its intersection with Route 539, is world famous for its pygmy pines

and oaks. Elsewhere in the Barrens, pitch pines, though scruffy, grow 40 feet tall. Here the pines and two species of oaks, packed together in dense forest, reach a maximum height of five to eight feet—and many mature trees are much shorter. For visitors, to look over the top of a forest canopy is an uncanny experience. The pines' inability to grow taller is one evolutionary adaptation to the frequent fires that are natural to the Pinelands ecosystem. The pines here have accommodated to the environment by developing underground trunks—lignotubers—that escape the ravages of flames and can weather repeated fire damage. Although the stems above ground may burn, new shoots arise from the lignotuber after a fire. Also, the cones of many pines do not open and shed seeds unless subjected to intense heat. Blackjack oaks (normally 25 to 30 feet tall) and scrub oaks in the vicinity have similarly evolved as midgets, as well as evolving the same lignotuber adaptation to fire.

West Pine Plains sustains a rich assortment of acid-loving shrubs: sheep laurel, dangleberry, *Hudsonia,* pyxie moss, and sand myrtle. The shrub component also includes one of the Barrens' rarest, broom crow-berry. The earliest bloomer in the Pinelands, appearing in February or March, the flower is inconspicuous to a fault and more curious than ravishing. Nevertheless, it is rare and usually found much farther north.

Wharton State Forest❖, on Route 542, includes the **Oswego River Natural Area❖,** a white cedar forest flanking the river. Drier portions present a mix of pine and oak, and the understory is a thicket of heath-type shrubs: blueberry, dangleberry (also called blue huckle-berry), leatherleaf, sweet pepperbush, and sheep laurel. Rare curly grass ferns grow on stumps of fallen cedars.

Many naturalists believe that the best way to enjoy the Pine Barrens is in a canoe. A narrow stream with a fairly swift current but no rapids, the **Mullica River❖** in Wharton is ideal for canoeing. One favorite course is the stretch between Atsion (locals say "At'zine") and Pleasant Mills, which the state of New Jersey has declared a wild and scenic river. Like all rivers in the Pinelands, the Mullica is the color of tea, a recipe concocted by nature from tannins in the cedar bark and the exposed bog iron in the bottom and banks of streams. Although the river is walled by green in a few spots, the prospect is generally more open, dotted with pitch pines, white cedars, and an abundance of acid-loving heath-type shrubs. High sandy banks frequently line the water, and dense stands of hardwoods rise at its upper end.

The Mullica also traverses savanna marshes, grassy plains where trees are uncommon. Here the banks are obscured by tall sedges and grasses and by shrubby thickets. In the river's lower segment, where open countryside is broken only occasionally by scattered pines and cedars, visitors frequently spot hawks circling overhead.

COASTAL MARSHES AND RIVERS

Just south of Long Beach Island, **Great Bay Boulevard Wildlife Management Area❖** on Seven Bridges Road outside Tuckerton is a mosaic of mudflats, salt marsh, and shallow ponds. Also known as Tuckerton Marsh, this elbow of land separates Little Egg Harbor and Great Bay; Great Bay Boulevard cuts through the middle of this little peninsula. The lushest part of the WMA's nearly 5,000 acres is a 500-acre salt marsh where a network of tidal creeks and open pools weave among hummocks carpeted with spartina grass. Loaded with crabs, mussels, and snails, the hummocks and waters are a prime attraction for shorebirds.

From early spring into fall, Great Bay Boulevard is one of the best spots in the Northeast to see American oystercatchers, which nest at Great Bay. Equipped with a bright orange bill that serves as a flat, heavy chisel, the oystercatcher jabs into mucky flats to uproot crabs, mollusks, and marine worms. When it finds a mussel, the bird inserts its bill between the tightly clamped shell halves and pries open the helpless mollusk. Visitors arriving early in the day often find flocks of oystercatchers noisily scurrying about, calling *wheep! wheep! wheep!* and probing. The large Great Bay shorebird cast includes whimbrels with long, curving beaks, various godwits, plover, and sandpipers. Ospreys nest and fish around here, and in fall shrubby thickets are packed with migrating songbirds.

The **Edwin B. Forsythe National Wildlife Refuge❖** is one of the jewels of this country's refuge system, not only because it shelters enormous numbers of birds in great variety—290 species recorded—but also because it is one of the most user-friendly refuges thanks to the auto tour that circles through the Brigantine division. Brigantine, the original refuge, was created in 1939 primarily to conserve estuarine habitats vital to the survival of brant, small, "formally attired" black, gray, and white geese; black ducks; several rail species; and migratory waterfowl in general. In 1967 the Fish and Wildlife Service established **Barnegat,** a second coastal refuge a few miles to the north, and some smaller parcels were added subsequently. All were combined under the Forsythe umbrella title in 1984, and the complex now totals about 40,000 acres. Birders almost always refer to the refuge as **Brigantine,** which with 24,000 acres is the biggest and most accessible unit (entrance on Great Creek Road in Oceanville, a mile east of Route 9).

Overall, 90 percent of Forsythe is tidal salt meadow and marsh covered with dense strands of cordgrass. Tucked amid the sprawl of tall grasses are shallow bays and coves. Tidal waters flowing through transform the habitat into spawning and feeding grounds and nurseries for awesome numbers of fish and shellfish, which then become a banquet for migratory birds. Wildlife managers have modified the habitat by creating two large artificial ponds called impoundments. One contains

LEFT: *Wild mustard flourishes in the Brigantine area of the Edwin B. Forsythe refuge.*

RIGHT: *In a freshwater marsh at Brigantine, a cattle egret in breeding plumage—pink crown and breast—wades through arrow arum.*

freshwater, the other brackish, a blend of fresh and salt water often found in estuaries. The ponds total 1,415 acres.

Brigantine's auto tour is an eight-mile one-way dirt-road loop that begins near the visitor center with salt marshes on the right and a freshwater pool on the left. In the latter, islands of vegetation divide the pond into winding aquatic channels and smaller pools. Early fall finds dabbling ducks—often called puddle ducks—feeding in these channels, tipping themselves tail up, head down to reach underwater vegetation, seeds, and snails. Mallard and blacks are most common, but plenty of northern shovelers, gadwalls, American wigeons, green-winged and blue-winged teal, and northern pintail appear as well. Great blue herons stalk the shallows with style and grace, freezing in position and then resuming their slow-motion locomotion; ultimately they thrust a swordlike beak into the water to snatch a fish that never knew what hit it. Around a bend in the reedy channel, a great egret approaches mealtime in much the same way, while snowy egrets pursue food in a more energetic, agitated fashion.

On flats and little grassy hummocks elevated above the water, groups of terns often gather to preen their feathers or rest. The tern species here are common and Forster's, black-capped birds with long, pointy black-tipped beaks. Around Turtle Cove on the marsh side, large aquatic diamondback terrapins, which nest here, peer from the water, showing distinctive white lip outlines.

In many places the marsh opens to reveal extensive mudflats exposed at low tide. Because the muck teems with tiny organisms delectable to shorebirds, the flats, shimmering in early autumn sunlight, attract crowds of greater and lesser yellowlegs, willets, sanderlings,

ABOVE: *"Running up the scale in a thin wiry voice"—as writer John Kieran once described it—a prairie warbler greets the day from a hickory tree.*

dunlins, dowitchers, and other sandpiper species. One or two Hudsonian and marbled godwits are occasionally seen. The birds strut about, poke their beaks into the mud, and occasionally flutter into the air like nervous grasshoppers.

Bushy clumps of grasses and weedy plants beside the road may be brimming with flocks of savannah or seaside sparrows seeking seeds. Along the backstretch of the auto loop long canals connect the pools, providing a great vantage point to watch black skimmers in action. A tern relative, the skimmer is a marvel of evolutionary engineering. The lower mandible of its distinctive red beak is about a third longer than the upper. As the skimmer flies just above the surface of a marshy channel, the lower bill slices through the water like a plow cutting a furrow. Once it touches a fish, the bill snaps shut, and the skimmer flies off to savor its meal. Around November, brant, snow geese, and Canada geese glide from the sky, blanketing Brigantine with thousands of feathered migrants. Added to the droves of ducks, they raise the waterfowl population to 150,000!

Early in the nineteenth century, the great naturalist and artist John James Audubon wrote, "Many a drawing I made at Great Egg Harbor, many a pleasant day I spent along its shores." He would no doubt be pleased that late in the twentieth century, the **Great Egg Harbor National Scenic and Recreational River**❖ became New Jersey's first to be so designated by the Wild and Scenic River System. Beginning in a

RIGHT: *Imported from Asia for its exquisite color and graceful form, lavender wisteria has naturalized extensively at the Brigantine refuge.*

swamp at Berlin (southeast of Camden), the Great Egg wiggles its way southeast to a bay opening on the Atlantic Ocean. Harbor and river were named by seventeenth-century Dutch colonists who found a bonanza of gull eggs in salt meadows around the bay in spring. The river is the longest canoeable stream in southern New Jersey and one of the cleanest in the state. Although the Great Egg can be canoed in its upper reaches, the waterway there is swampy, narrow, and often choked by debris.

The most popular run is between the villages of Penny Pot and Weymouth, an easy six-mile day trip. Because the river's watershed is part of the Pinelands, its water is tea-colored, a by-product of dissolving iron in the soil and tannin from cedar trees. Edged by tall, sandy banks, the Great Egg meanders slowly under an open sky. Among scattered pines and scrub oaks grow blueberry and huckleberry shrubs, and stands of holly and mountain laurel often line the banks. North of Weymouth, groves of cedar trees tower above the shore. Surprise encounters with deer and raccoon are more likely than encounters with people, and really fortunate travelers may round a bend to discover otters playing in the river.

Major portions of the **Maurice National Scenic and Recreational River❖** and three of its tributaries received federal wild and scenic river designation in 1993, the second such listing in New Jersey. Locally the name is pronounced Morris, and it's best seen from the water. Before the river empties into Delaware Bay, the most scenic section wriggles through a marshy area stretching from Millville south to Mauricetown, a restored historic village picturesque in its own right.

Canoeing, which is possible on the northern portions of the Maurice, where it is fairly narrow and travels through red maple swamp forest, is not advisable on the lower section. Here the river, often 150 yards wide and strongly tidal, is best approached in a small boat powered by an outboard motor. When the tidewater is high, the salt marsh alongside the river is easier to see.

During June riverbanks blush with countless mountain laurel blossoms. Vast fields of wild rice fill the marsh with hundreds of red-

---

Left: *At the height of its mating display, a male great egret curls its neck and raises its feathery plumes to attract a female. The bright green stripe between its eye and bill only appears during breeding season.*

239

winged blackbirds, their tomato-red shoulder epaulets flaring competitively in summer sunlight. As they chow down on rice seeds, these feathered gluttons fill the air with buzzing calls that sound like a warehouse full of doorbells out of control. Nesting among the cattails and grasses are many birds, including soras and other rail, which are heard but seldom seen. Ospreys nest here—on both natural and artificial platforms—and patrol the river for a bass or perch dinner for themselves and new offspring.

A little south of Millville, sandy bluffs rise 20 to 30 feet above the river's edge. Crowds of bank swallows dart from their nesting holes in the bluffs to grab passing insects, while great blue herons and egrets pace the shallows along gravelly banks and in the marsh, searching for tasty meals. Belted kingfishers streak like blue lightning from cliff-side burrows to pluck small fish from the waters below, and tree swallows, mimicking their bank-dwelling cousins, retire to hollow trees with their insect catch. Roughly opposite the tall bluffs, mudflats at low tide are filled with invertebrate life—mussels, blue and soft-shell crabs, fiddler crabs, clams, oysters, snails—providing a rich wildlife menu on both sides of the river.

From late September until well into November, this stretch of the Maurice is beak-to-beak with great rafts of waterfowl—thousands of northern pintail, green-winged and blue-winged teal, mallard, and black ducks. The boater encounters a dramatic sight indeed when a flock of ducks, following signals unseen by humans, suddenly drift down to the water and begin paddling as one, not missing a beat. Autumn is also splendid for sightings of migrating raptors, especially large numbers of broad-winged hawks. During the relatively mild winters, the river and its banks attract the largest congregation of bald eagles in the state.

Cape May

"If birds are good judges of excellent climate, Cape May has the finest climate in the United States, for it has the greatest variety of birds," wrote Alexander Wilson, the father of American ornithology, about 1810. A pleasing climate is only one factor in the cape's avian abundance, but

RIGHT: *Near a sandy bluff, East Point Lighthouse perches at the edge of Maurice River Cove. Feeding into Delaware Bay, the Maurice nourishes an ecosystem rich in fish, aquatic plants, invertebrates, and birdlife.*

Many species of wading birds visit the Cape May area each year, including the smallish green heron (left), the larger yellow-crowned night heron (above), and the stout-bodied American oystercatcher (near right). Seabirds include the clamorous laughing gull (top right) and the imposing double-crested cormorant (far right).

Wilson was merely stating what nearly two additional centuries of observation and research have confirmed: Cape May is the premier birding hot spot in North America. By any standard—total numbers, species diversity, pageantry of natural spectacle—Cape May has the edge.

The name Cape May can mean several things. Most tourists picture the charming old resort town filled with gingerbready Victorian houses. Others envision the peninsula, which projects south between the Atlantic Ocean and Delaware Bay. When birders speak of Cape May, however (and 100,000 of them visit each year), they mean the whole region—the town, the county of the same name, and areas that overlap into neighboring counties as well.

The birds come largely because of circumstances beyond their control. Traveling south in autumn, millions of migratory birds follow two traditional highways—the Atlantic Coast and the Delaware River valley. Raptors utilize a special corridor shaped by mountain ridges where winds give them a boost. In all cases, as the prevailing northwesterly winds of autumn shoo the birds southward, they naturally follow New Jersey's peninsular shape until they literally funnel down to the southernmost tip, Cape May. When suddenly confronted by 12 miles of open water at Delaware Bay, they put on the brakes, stack up, and regroup in

great concentrations. As they wait for winds to give them a lift across the bay and on to the next leg of their journey, the birds rest and feed at Cape May. Reversing the process in spring, they reach this little wedge of land after an arduous flight over water and again pause to rest and regain strength. For its part, the Cape is exceedingly hospitable, providing an unusual diversity of biologically rich habitats that support species of all sorts. The location is also attractive to birders because so much of the area is open countryside where birds are easily sighted.

Although they cannot be counted precisely, the number of birds passing through is in the millions. Tallying species is easier: 402 as of this writing. Another 70 species spotted within a hundred miles of Cape May will probably be added to the roster sooner or later. At least 350 species are annual visitors. The greatest numbers appear during fall migration, which on the bird calendar runs from June 23 to January 10. Spring migration begins January 10 and continues through June 10. Thus lots of birds are always on hand, even in the winter. The annual Christmas bird count averages more than 130 species, and the total of individual birds often exceeds 200,000.

Beginning in the northwest corner of the county, **Belleplain State Forest**❖ on Route 550 includes some 13,000 acres of pine-oak forest,

LEFT: *The stillness of a pine and hard-wood forest in the Dennis Creek Wildlife Management Area is broken only by rustling leaves and bird calls.*
RIGHT: *This robust woodchuck has amassed a solid layer of fat to see it through the winter, when it hiber-nates in a carefully prepared burrow.*

white cedar swamps, mixed hard-wood forest, and several ponds. In most areas of the forest, trees can be scanned from roads. The greatest species diversity occurs around white cedars along stream banks. May and June yield a bevy of breed-ing birds, notably warblers: yellow-throated, pine, prairie, blue-winged, worm-eating, black-and-white, hood-ed, parula, prothonotary, ovenbirds, Louisiana waterthrushes, as well as eastern phoebes and Acadian flycatchers. Bald eagles can be observed and actively nest here. The forest is harvested, and even clear-cut areas afford bird sightings: red-headed woodpeckers, brown thrashers, blue-birds, wild turkeys, grouse, broad-winged hawks, and more.

A few miles southeast on the Atlantic coast, the pleasant resort com-munity of **Avalon** projects a mile into the ocean, giving land-bound ob-servers the closest possible view of the 500,000–600,000 seabirds that travel near shore in the fall. (The 1994 watch recorded 641,035.) The cast is quite varied: double-crested cormorants and common and red-throat-ed loons repeatedly diving under the waves in search of food; black-legged kittiwakes, oceanic gulls hoisted by wind to hover above the sea; sea ducks called scoters (white-winged, black, and surf) that collect in groups to ride the waves. Occasionally a large gray bird with long points extending from its tail may be seen harassing gulls and terns; this terror-ist is probably a parasitic jaeger trying to make another bird cough up its fish dinner. Seabirds the size of big geese, northern gannets are com-mon—100,000 may wing through in a season. Gannets sweep the sky, then plummet like white bricks, headfirst, into the ocean once they spot fish. Brown pelicans perform in similar fashion, circling gracefully above and then plunging seaward, their long bills knifing into the water. This activity peaks from October 1 through November 30, and the best viewing is from a small parking lot on Avalon's Eighth Street jetty; Seventh Street is a good second choice. A telescope is desirable.

The largest heron rookery in southern New Jersey occupies **Sedge Island❖,** off the town of Stone Harbor. Although the area is visible from the end of 114th Street, tour boats provide a closer look. Follow Third Avenue south from Stone Harbor to a causeway that runs through **Nummy Island❖,** a large salt marsh where yellow-crowned night herons, stout gray birds with plumes sweeping back from a yellow-and-white cap, feed along with other herons and egrets. The island is a feeding-nesting site for many shorebirds, including oystercatchers, Hudsonian and marbled godwits, and Wilson's and red-necked phalaropes. The handsome phalaropes are energetic feeders, sometimes spinning around in shallow water to stir up tiny invertebrates, then plucking them from the soupy liquid. **Ring Island** to the northwest cannot be visited, but from Nummy visitors can see at least some members of the largest laughing gull colony in the state—10,000 pairs.

Because it is a critical nesting site for scores of endangered and threatened species, **Champagne Island,** in Hereford Inlet between Stone Harbor and North Wildwood, is strictly off limits to people. The state's largest colony of black skimmers (500 pairs) nest here, along with 1,000 common tern pairs, piping plover, and clapper rail. During fall migration (beginning mid-July), shorebirds abound: whimbrels, red knots, dunlins, dowitchers, semipalmated and black-bellied plover, least and semipalmated sandpipers, greater and lesser yellowlegs, and terns—as many as 2,000 individuals of seven species at one time. With a telescope, these multitudes are visible from a seawall on Anglesea Drive in North Wildwood, and a boat tour offers a closer view.

Southern New Jersey's near-shore waters have become the whale-watching capital of the Mid-Atlantic. Based in Cape May Harbor, a number of wildlife-watching boats generally travel 15 to 18 miles out. June and July are best for spotting large cetaceans. Human voyagers invariably experience an adrenalin surge when they hear the soft explosion of air and mist that a humpback whale makes as it surfaces and exhales. Nearly 40 feet long, the mottled charcoal-gray Goliath arches its broad back slowly and gracefully, then slips silently below the surface again, its giant tail flukes seeming to wave good-bye before disappearing. Even more exhilarating are the rare occasions when a humpback erupts completely out of the water, propelling itself straight up like a NASA spacecraft, then crashing back into the ocean. Although it suggests cetacean friskiness, the behavior, called breaching, isn't fully understood.

Humpbacks are usually encountered on these trips, though sightings cannot be guaranteed. Fin whales and pilot whales often appear, and occasionally right whales do. Visitors frequently make the acquaintance of a group of bottle-nosed dolphins, leaping above the waves like circus acrobats. Spotted dolphins and harbor porpoises also pass regularly. On lucky days, a sea turtle can be seen basking at the surface, a shark cruising by, or a gigantic ocean sunfish—seemingly all head and dorsal fins—floating placidly on the waves.

An added bonus is the sight of pelagic, or open ocean, birds, which spend major parts of their lives at sea. Good possibilities are several shearwater species (Cory's, greater, Manx, and sooty), gull-sized gray birds with tubular nostrils atop their hooked beaks. On extended pointed wings, they glide just above the waves—sometimes between swells—now and then dipping down to skim a fish from the sea. Wilson's storm petrels, close but much smaller relatives, also frequent the neighborhood. Charcoal with a white crescent on the tail, they are skittery flyers, fluttering inches above the water and daintily dancing feetfirst over waves to snare little fish.

Many bird lovers head straight for the tip of the peninsula and the lighthouse in **Cape May Point State Park❖**, a 200-acre land's end that draws a wealth of birds. On one notable September day, birders here toted up 119 species. Right next door to the park is New Jersey Audubon's **Cape May Bird Observatory❖**, which offers birders invaluable information on birding throughout the region and maintains a birding hotline providing the latest scoop on what birds are where. From late August to early October, thousands and thousands of tree swallows—to cite one example—perch on telephone wires like lustrous blue-green beads strung on a necklace around the park.

In addition to its ideal location, the park compresses within a relatively small space a variety of habitats: sand dunes, beach, coastal ponds, freshwater marsh, and woodlands. A three-mile network of marked trails meander through the lot. In the fall, visitors can stroll

down the beach to ponds laced with cattails and reeds and start checking off ducks, gulls, herons, egrets, and shorebirds. Smaller birds such as sedge wrens perch on the reeds.

Least bitterns are fairly common, but these small buff-colored herons with black caps and wing tips are so secretive that they are rarely seen—although their cuckoolike calls are often heard. Bitterns nesting around these ponds, however, appear regularly in spring and summer. Follow trails through woody thickets of bayberry, black cherry, sassafras, and sweet gum to seek migrating songbirds.

During autumn, birds of prey stream through the park in staggering numbers. New Jersey Audubon conducts its annual hawk watch at the point from August 15 through December 1. (In spring, migrating hawks are more widely dispersed, and their numbers are smaller at Cape May.) Hawk watchers are aided by an elevated platform that provides unobstructed views north and east. The census here averages 50,000 raptors annually, and the estimated total for all of Cape May is 200,000 a year. At peak times, anyone spending a ten-hour day on the platform can easily see several thousand hawks. Fifteen raptor species visit regularly, usually beginning with ospreys and kestrels in August. Golden and bald eagles appear later in the fall. The most numerous species are sharp-shinned hawks, American kestrels, and Cooper's and red-tailed hawks. Broad-winged hawks are also common. Large flights of owls—principally saw-whet, barn, and long-eared—also pass the point in autumn.

One of the delights of Cape May is that geography and weather (not to mention luck) cause accidentals—birds that have strayed off course far from their usual haunts, usually thousands of miles—to appear with some frequency. The high percentage of accidentals landing here includes whiskered terns (common in Eurasia, but seen in North America only at Cape May); scissor-tailed flycatchers (more likely on the plains of Texas and Oklahoma); cave swallows from the West Indies; Bell's vireos from mid-America and the Southwest; wood storks, seldom seen north of the Deep South; and from America's Far West, rock wrens and Say's phoebes. Although these vagrants can show up

LEFT: *Encircled by grasses and sand, the pond at Cape May Point State Park is a prime birding spot. The dunes protect ponds and marshes from the sea, which has recently eroded a small portion of Cape May.*

in any season, the most likely time seems to be the first week of November, also known as Wild Card Week.

Adjacent to the park along its eastern border is the **William D. and June C. Blair Cape May Migratory Bird Refuge❖,** a 187-acre Nature Conservancy preserve. Less woodsy than the park, this weedy, seaside meadow is dotted with shallow brackish and freshwater ponds, and marshy vegetation flanks its eastern edge. During fall migration, it is often one of the finest spots in the region to see a broad assortment of plover, sandpipers, dowitchers, godwits, and phalaropes—15 to 20 shorebird species. It becomes especially entertaining when peregrines, kestrels, and merlins—streamlined speed demons all—torment the shorebirds at high speed. In summer, egrets, herons, and rail strut around the marshy ponds. Gulls are here year-round, along with a sizable tern colony. Naturalists have identified nearly a hundred species of dragonflies and damselflies frequenting Cape May, and this refuge is one of the best places to see them in summer and early fall.

DELAWARE BAY

A few miles north along Delaware Bay, at the end of New England Road, **Higbee Beach Wildlife Management Area❖** is the most popular spot in the region for bird enthusiasts, especially in autumn. Behind a beach extending a mile and a half along the bay, nature and man have blended sand dunes, woodlands, weedy fields, prickly hedgerows, and freshwater ponds and meadows in a 634-acre sanctuary. This is Songbird City, and most of the 200 species recorded at Cape May show up here.

The moments of high drama, called fallouts, usually occur from mid-August through October after a combination of cold front, clear skies, and northwest winds have driven great flights of birds down the coast. At daybreak, they suddenly find themselves at the peninsula or over open ocean. Exhausted, they battle back against the wind, retreating to a low dune forest at Higbee Beach. The forest is a tangle of holly trees, red-cedars, pitch pines, black cherries, beach plum, bayberry, and persimmon trees, their weathered branches contorted by winds and enveloped

---

RIGHT: *A marsh abuts the sandy beach trail at the Cape May bird refuge. Nineteenth-century naturalist Alexander Wilson identified two significant species nearby, the Cape May warbler and Wilson's plover.*

in Virginia creeper, wild grape, and poison ivy. Literally tens of thousands of little birds drop into the woods, swarming over the branches like clouds of insects as they scramble to find perches. They are so dense that sometimes their wings tickle the faces of onlookers, and even experienced birders have difficulty identifying the moving targets.

The fallout phenomenon occurs mostly in fall, but spring fallouts can be even more dazzling because the birds are in breeding plumage. As a deluge of warblers rain from the sky, gaps in the greenery seem to dance with shards of stained glass in the world's largest kaleidoscope. The most magical time is the hour after dawn, although big flights continue most of the morning as birds seek cover in fields and hedgerows, and the best vantage point is the dike along the Cape May Canal at the north end of the refuge. Although massive fallouts occur on only a handful of days during the year, hordes of songbirds appear regularly. The greatest diversity of species occurs in mid-August, when warblers begin arriving, and September and October boast the biggest numbers.

Hawks too stop at Higbee in autumn. Species that rely on strong air currents to speed them on their way dislike long flights over water, where such help is minimal. Thus broad-winged, red-tailed, and red-shouldered hawks screech to a halt when they reach Cape May Point. In frustration, they retreat north along the bay seeking a narrower, less forbidding passage and roost overnight in Higbee forests. Just after dawn, the sky is filled with soaring raptors.

About 60 percent of all woodcocks hatched in the Northeast pass through Cape May, and the open fields at Higbee Beach are loaded with them in spring and fall. Their springtime courtship is a special treat. Peak activity is in early March—the ritual continues into April—and the best time is twilight. Visitors inevitably hear woodcocks first—a nasal *peent!*—because their camouflaging plumage renders them invisible in the weedy vegetation. The cock leaps up from the ground and begins spiraling upward in ever-widening arcs, making a twittering sound with his furiously beating wings. When he reaches about 300

LEFT: *On Higbee Beach, a Virginia creeper vine and a dying cherry tree cling to a windswept sand dune overlooking Delaware Bay. Fighting powerful gusts, countless migrating birds use this beach as a rest stop.*

ABOVE: *Long-necked Canada geese and laughing gulls intently search for morsels of food in a tidal pool along New Jersey's Atlantic coast.*

feet, he hovers briefly while chirping, then embarks on a zigzag descent, swooping and looping like a feather caught on the wind, wings whistling as he drops. After landing, he goose-steps to a waiting female, and if his performance has been up to her standards, they mate.

From late spring through fall, the same fields vibrate with butterflies—blue, green, orange, yellow, red, brown, purple, white—fluttering amid the grasses and sipping nectar from wildflowers. The multihued cast is equally diverse in size: big ones like black, spicebush, and tiger swallowtails; moderates like mourning cloaks; small ones like clouded sulphurs; and tiny critters like red-banded hairstreaks. Of the 104 species around the cape, most are found at Higbee Beach. Hundreds of orange-and-black monarchs are autumn transients bound for winter havens in the South and Mexico.

Higbee Beach is one of the best places to find Cape May diamonds,

RIGHT: *At Cape May, carapaces of two male horseshoe crabs are memorials to the tumultuous mating rituals that unfold here each spring.*

pebbles of clear quartz with a sparkle suggestive of gemstone but in fact with little value. They're tarted up with chemical colors and sold in shops, but at the beach they're free and clear.

About 10 miles north, the **Dennis Creek Wildlife Management Area❖,** on Jakes Landing Road off Route 47, is mostly salt marsh. In spring and summer, this WMA is a prime location for spotting nesting birds not easily seen elsewhere: Virginia, clapper, and king rails, marsh wrens, yellow-throated warblers, and a large variety of duck species. Winter brings an opportunity to observe short-eared owls, northern harriers, and bald eagles with relative ease. Where the marsh meets Delaware Bay, thousands and thousands of snow geese gather.

Every year, when the waters of Delaware Bay warm up and the days grow longer early in May, beaches along the bay are transformed into Triassic Park as a prehistoric ritual unfolds. For many people, the spectacle is an essential part of the Cape May experience. Hundreds of thousands of horseshoe crabs, looking like Darth Vader helmets with legs and long spiky tails, creep out of the sea to commence their annual mating rites. As the tide begins lowering, males form a massive phalanx in the surf. When tidewater recedes a little more, the larger females emerge, plowing their way through a battalion of ardent suitors while as many as five males attempt to link up with a single female. Using appendages evolved for just this moment, one of the contending males succeeds eventually, locking on and riding her domed back toward the high-water mark.

Each female lays 50,000 to 80,000 greenish brown eggs the size of BB shot, spreading them around in batches of about 4,000. She deposits them in sandy depressions two to eight inches deep, sometimes in several layers. After her clinging partner fertilizes them, the eggs are buried, and the happy couple return to the sea, often still joined. The orgy leaves many males flipped over on their backs. Thousands expire every year, victims of their own libidos.

The players are not crabs; they are biologically closer to arachnids such as spiders and scorpions. Horseshoes have their own order but only four species, three of them Asian. The line originated about 570 million years ago in the Cambrian era, and the species that cavorts on Delaware Bay is essentially the same as one that crawled out of Triassic oceans 250 million years ago. As many as three to four million horseshoes are estimated to participate in this pilgrimage. After a month of such activity, billions of eggs are sunk in sands along the bay. Few remain there for long.

Taking their cue from internal body clocks, changes of day length, and other signals, epic numbers of shorebirds commence migratory flights from South America, traveling 2,000 to 4,000 miles nonstop. Arriving at Delaware Bay, they are exhausted and famished, having lost half their body weight on the trip. Showering down on beaches, they devour the horseshoe crab eggs, lending new meaning to the phrase "feeding frenzy." Each bird spends ten days to two weeks wolfing down thousands of tiny eggs per day. Scientists estimate that 25 billion eggs are consumed, about 100 tons. Fortified, their body weight doubled, the birds take off for breeding grounds in the Arctic tundra, another nonstop journey of about 3,000 miles.

Every year half a million to a million shorebirds blanket the beaches; in some years, an estimated 1.5 million. Approximately 20 species partake of the feast, but 4 are most numerous. Virtually the entire North American population of red knots—150,000 to 200,000 birds—stop at Delaware Bay. They constitute 80 percent of the world population of these chunky chestnut-colored birds, which are among the first gluttons in line for eggs each year. They are joined by 50 percent of the Western Hemisphere's Atlantic sanderling population, half of North America's ruddy turnstones, and enormous numbers of semipalmated sandpipers.

The event begins in early May, reaching its awesome climax May 18–28 in most years, and ending around June 10. Outgoing tide is the optimum time for observers because the eggs are more exposed. Of the several beaches in New Jersey and Delaware where this phenomenon may be seen, **Reed's Beach❖** (on County Road 655 off Route 47) is one of the best for bird numbers and accessibility. A public beach and a viewing platform are at the north end of the road. Visitors to Reed's Beach can easily see 5,000 red knots in a single day, not to mention the other species. This event—one of the greatest wildlife spectacles in North America—is a main reason why Cape May is called the Birding Capital of America.

OVERLEAF: *Filling both water and sky, migrating pintail gather at sunset. Waterfowl generally migrate in daylight; some species travel both day and night, using different calls when navigating in darkness.*

FURTHER READING ABOUT THE MID-ATLANTIC STATES

BARNETT, LINCOLN. *The Ancient Adirondacks.* New York: Time-Life Books, 1974. The sights, sounds, smells, and feelings experienced by a sensitive outdoorsman and author awed by the grandeur and beauty of the Adirondacks.

BERKELEY, EDMUND, AND DOROTHY SMITH BERKELEY. *The Life and Travels of John Bartram: From Lake Ontario to the River of St. John.* Tallahassee: University Presses of Florida, 1982. A detailed biography that follows the far-flung wanderings of America's first great botanist, a brilliant, self-taught Quaker farmer from Philadelphia.

BOYD, HOWARD P. *A Field Guide to the Pine Barrens of New Jersey.* Medford, NJ: Plexus Publishing, 1991. This volume covers geology, climate, flora, fauna—all the natural ingredients that make the Pinelands an exotic, world-renowned wetland. It also includes doses of human history and culture.

BOYLE, WILLIAM J., JR. *A Guide to Bird Finding in New Jersey.* New Brunswick, NJ: Rutgers University Press, 1986. Indispensable for anyone on the Jersey birding beat, this guide covers more than 70 sites from the Highlands to Cape May.

DRENNAN, SUSAN RONEY. *Where to Find Birds in New York State.* Syracuse, NY: Syracuse University Press, 1981. A comprehensive guide to more than 500 sites in every corner of the Empire State.

HARDING, JOHN J., ED. *Marsh, Meadow, Mountain.* Philadelphia: Temple University Press, 1986. Nine naturalists describe the high points of seven ecological regions within the Delaware Valley of Pennsylvania and New Jersey.

JEROME, CHRISTINE. *An Adirondack Passage.* New York: Harper Collins, 1994. A lyrical account of a month-long voyage by canoe that retraced an 1883 exploration, traveling 266 miles from Boonville to Paul Smiths, almost the entire length of the Adirondacks. The author discovers happily that relatively little has changed along the route in more than a century.

KICK, PETER, BARBARA MCMARTIN, AND JAMES M. LONG. *Fifty Hikes in the Hudson Valley.* Woodstock, VT: Countryman Press, 1994. Although it is on the edge of major population centers, the Hudson River valley offers wondrous walking through small but exquisite mountain ranges: the Catskills, Taconics, Shawangunks, Ramapos, Helderbergs, and more.

LAWRENCE, SUSANNAH, AND BARBARA GROSS. *The Audubon Society Field Guide to the Natural Places of the Mid-Atlantic States: Inland.* New York: Pantheon, 1984. In an unorthodox, ecologically oriented approach to touring the region, the authors delve into a broad variety of natural phenomena that help readers understand and appreciate the area's scenic wonders. A second, similar volume explores coastal areas.

MCPHEE, JOHN. *The Pine Barrens.* New York: Farrar, Straus and Giroux, 1968. One of America's most eloquent nature writers examines the Pineland's natural and human history.

OPLINGER, CARL, AND ROBERT HALMA. *Poconos: An Illustrated Natural History.* New Brunswick, NJ: Rutgers University Press, 1988. This extensively illustrated volume discusses the origins of the mountains' geological features, as well as the region's plant and animal life and the current status of these natural aspects.

ROSEBERRY, C. R. *From Niagara to Montauk.* Albany: State University of New York Press, 1982. Emphasizing scenic splendor and historical associations, a geologist interprets more than 60 of New York's best-known scenic glories.

SCOFIELD, BRUCE, STELLA J. GREEN, AND H. NEIL ZIMMERMAN. *Fifty Hikes in New Jersey.* Woodstock, VT: Backcountry Publications, 1993. Getting off the highways and away from dense human population, the authors outline a surprising abundance of beautiful treks through the Garden State.

SNYDER, BRADLEY. *The Shawangunk Mountains.* New Paltz, NY: The Mohonk Preserve, 1981. The author discusses the history of some enchanted mountains and the people who live among them.

THWAITES, TOM. *Fifty Hikes in Western Pennsylvania* and *Fifty Hikes in Central Pennsylvania.* Woodstock, VT: Countryman Press, 1990 and 1995, respectively. Provides explicit directions on how to enjoy two thirds of the Keystone State on foot.

VAN DIVER, BRADFORD B. *Roadside Geology of New York* and *Roadside Geology of Pennsylvania.* Missoula, MT: Mountain Press Publishing, 1985 and 1990, respectively. For rock hounds (or anyone with a more than passing interest in nature), these guides turn highways and backroads into entertaining, instructive theaters of the ages.

ABOVE: *In the late 1800s, sportsmen built rustic camps in the Adirondacks, and the area's popularity aided its preservation. In 1895 the Inman camp on Raquette Lake boasted a honeymoon cottage with attached lean-to.*

GLOSSARY

alpine pertaining to mountain zones of extremely high elevation

aquifer underground layer of porous, water-bearing rock, sand, or gravel

barrier island narrow island made of sediment—sand, silt, and gravel—that protects the coast from direct battering by storm waves and winds

biotic pertaining to plants and animals

bog wetland, formed in glacial kettle holes, common to cool climates of northern North America, Europe, and Asia; acidic nature produces large quantities of peat moss

boreal relating to the northern biotic area characterized especially by the dominance of coniferous forests

brackish referring to salty or briny water, particularly a mixture of fresh and salt water found in estuaries

climax forest ecological forest community that has reached the hypothetical condition of evolutionary stability in which all successional changes in the community have taken place

conglomerate rock composed of rounded waterworn fragments of older rock, usually in combination with sand

coniferous describing the cone-bearing trees of the pine family; usually evergreen

deciduous referring to plants that shed their leaves seasonally and are leafless for part of the year

drumlin hill of glacial debris that was smoothed by overriding ice into the shape of an overturned spoon

escarpment cliff or steep rock face, formed by faulting or fracturing of the earth's crust, that separates two comparatively level land surfaces

esker long, winding rise of gravel and sand that marks the trail where a river once flowed beneath a glacier

estuary region of interaction between ocean water and the end of a river, where tidal action and river flow mix fresh and salt water

gneiss foliated, coarse-grained metamorphic rock similar in composition to granite

kame cone-shaped hill of rock debris deposited by glacial meltwater

kettle hole glacial depression that, when fed by groundwater and precipitation, often evolves into a bog

microclimate small, local area of usually uniform temperature, humidity, and precipitation

moraine debris (rock, sand, gravel, silt, and clay) carried by a glacier and left along its sides or terminus wherever it pauses or retreats

peat partially decayed, spongy plant matter that makes up much of the substance of bogs; considered the first stage in the transformation of plant material into coal

plate thick slab of rock that makes up the earth's outer shell, including the ocean floor and the continental land masses; movement and interaction of the plates is known as plate tectonics

pothole bowl-shaped depression left by chunk of glacial ice buried in soil; when the ice melts, water fills the pothole, creating either a lake or a marsh

rapids broken, fast-flowing water that tumbles around boulders; classified from I to VI according to increasing difficulty of watercraft navigation

sandstone sedimentary rock composed of sand grains

scarp line of steep cliffs formed by erosion

sedimentary referring to rocks formed from deposits of eroded debris such as gravel, sand, mud, silt, or peat

shale sedimentary rock composed mainly of clay or other fine material

sphagnum moss that grows in wet, acidic areas; decomposes and compacts to form peat

stalactite icicle-shaped piece of dripstone formed on the roof of a cave when water containing dissolved limestone drips and evaporates, leaving the mineral formation

stalagmite spire formed on a cave floor when water drips and deposits minerals that had been dissolved in the water

subclimax forest ecological forest community unable to evolve naturally due to outside factors such as repeated fires or logging

talus rock debris that accumulates at the base of a cliff

tectonic referring to the deformation of the earth's crust, the forces involved, and the resulting formations

till unsorted rock debris, usually of a wide range of sizes, deposited directly from glacial ice without reworking by streams

tundra cold region characterized by low-level vegetation dominated by lichens, mosses, and low-growing vascular plants; exists as alpine zone of mountain ranges in lower latitudes, or arctic zone of polar areas in the far north

wetland area of land covered or saturated with groundwater; includes swamps, marshes, and bogs

ABOVE: *Hikers once dressed for a woodland outing a bit differently than trekkers do today. This 1903 group portrait, preserved on glass plate, was done at Leatherstocking Falls near Cooperstown, New York.*

LAND MANAGEMENT RESOURCES

The following public and private organizations are among the important administrators of the preserved and protected areas described in this volume. Brief explanations of the various legal and legislative designations of these areas follow.

MANAGING ORGANIZATIONS

Adirondack Park Agency
New York State agency that regulates use of the 3.4 million acres of private land within Adirondack Park. Administers state Wild, Scenic, and Recreational Rivers Act and Freshwater Wetlands Act in the park.

National Park Service (NPS) Department of the Interior
Regulates the use of national parks, monuments, and preserves. Resources are managed to preserve and protect landscape, natural and historic artifacts, and wildlife. Also administers historic and national landmarks, national seashores, wild and scenic rivers, and the national trail system.

The Nature Conservancy (TNC) Private organization
International nonprofit organization that owns the largest private system of nature sanctuaries in the world, some 1,300 preserves. Aims to preserve significant and diverse plants, animals, and natural communities

New Jersey Audubon Society Private organization
Independent, nonprofit conservation organization that owns 26 sanctuaries for wildlife and native flora, especially endangered and threatened species.

New Jersey Division of Fish, Game, and Wildlife
Manages 91 wildlife management areas occupying 225,415 acres. Areas are managed for hunting, fishing, and conservation. Regulates state hunting and fishing licenses. Part of Department of Environmental Protection.

New Jersey Division of Parks and Forestry
Manages 37 state parks, 42 natural areas, 57 historic sites, 11 state forests, and 4 recreation areas. Part of Division of Environmental Protection.

New York State Department of Environmental Conservation
Established to conserve state's natural resources and environment. Oversees Divisions of Fish and Wildlife, Lands and Forests, and Marine Resources.

New York State Office of Parks, Recreation, and Historic Preservation
Administers 151 state parks, preserves, and recreational facilities and 35 state historic sites.

Pennsylvania Bureau of Forestry
Administers 2.1 million acres of 20 state forests for conservation, timber, and recreation. Part of Department of Conservation and Natural Resources.

Pennsylvania Bureau of State Parks
Manages 116 state parks and 4 environmental education areas totaling 282,500 acres for recreation and education. Part of Department of Conservation and Natural Resources.

U.S. Fish and Wildlife Service (USFWS) Department of the Interior
Principal federal agency responsible for conserving, protecting, and en-

hancing the country's fish and wildlife and their habitats. Manages national wildlife refuges and fish hatcheries as well as programs for migratory birds and endangered and threatened species.

U.S. Forest Service (USFS) Department of Agriculture
Administers more than 190 million acres in the national forests and national grasslands. Determines how best to combine commercial uses such as grazing, mining, and logging with conservation needs.

DESIGNATIONS

National Forest
Large acreage managed for the use of forests, watersheds, wildlife, and recreation by the public and private sectors. Managed by the USFS.

National Recreation Area
Site established to conserve and develop for recreational purposes an area of scenic, natural, or historic interest. Powerboats, dirt and mountain bikes, and ORVs allowed with restrictions. Managed by the NPS.

National Seashore
Area of pristine, undeveloped seashore designated to protect its natural value and provide public recreation. Camping and ORVs allowed with restrictions. Managed by the NPS.

National Wildlife Refuge
Public land set aside for wild animals; protects migratory waterfowl, endangered and threatened species, and native plants. Managed by USFWS.

Natural Area
Area preserved in its natural state for its exceptional value in displaying the natural history of the United States. Managed by individual states.

Nature Preserve
Area that protects specific natural resources. Hunting, fishing, and mining may be permitted. Managed by the NPS and local or state authorities.

Wild and Scenic River System
National program set up to preserve selected rivers in their natural, free-flowing condition; stretches are classified as wild, scenic, or recreational, depending on the degree of development along the river, shoreline, or adjacent lands. Management shared by BLM, NPS, and USFWS.

Wilderness Area
Area with particular ecological, geological, scientific, scenic, or historical value that has been set aside in its natural condition to be strictly preserved as wild lands; limited recreational use is permitted. Managed by BLM and NPS.

Wildlife Management Area
Land managed or owned by the state to protect wildlife. Aside from seasonal restrictions, hunting, fishing, and public access are allowed. Managed by individual states.

NATURE TRAVEL

The following is a selection of national and local organizations that sponsor nature-related travel activities or can provide specialized regional travel information.

NATIONAL

National Audubon Society
700 Broadway
New York, NY 10003
(212) 979-3000
Offers a wide range of ecological field studies, tours, and cruises throughout the United States

National Wildlife Federation
1400 16th St. NW
Washington, D.C. 20036
(703) 790-4363
Offers training in environmental education, wildlife camp and teen adventures, conservation summits with nature walks, field trips, and classes

The Nature Conservancy
1815 North Lynn Street
Arlington, VA 22209
(703) 841-5300
Offers a variety of excursions from regional and state offices. May include hiking, backpacking, canoeing, horseback riding. Call to locate state offices

Sierra Club Outings
85 2nd St., 2nd floor
San Francisco, CA 94105
(415) 977-5630
Offers tours of different lengths for all ages throughout the United States. Outings may include backpacking, hiking, biking, skiing, and water excursions

Smithsonian Study Tours and Seminars
1100 Jefferson Dr. SW, MRC 702
Washington, DC 20560
(202) 357-4700
Offers extended tours, cruises, research expeditions, and seminars throughout the United States

REGIONAL

The Adirondack Mountain Club, Inc.
814 Goggins Rd.
Lake George, NY 12845
(518) 668-4447
Twenty-six chapters in New York and New Jersey sponsor activities such as canoe trips, hiking, climbing, and skiing

Audubon Council of Pennsylvania
1104 Fernwood Ave., #300
Camp Hill, PA 17011
(717) 763-4985
Central office of Pennsylvania's National Audubon Society chapters. Nonprofit conservation organization conducts nature programs including walks, hikes, and canoe trips. Call for reservations

New Jersey Division of Travel and Tourism
20 West State St.
Trenton, NJ 08625
(609) 292-2470 (specific questions)
(800) JERSEY 7 (537-7397) (travel literature)
Call for specific information or to request maps, state travel guides, and calendars

New York State Division of Tourism
1 Commerce Plaza
Albany, NY 12245
(800) 225-5697
Publishes state travel guide; answers phone queries about nature travel and accommodations

Pennsylvania Office of Travel and Tourism
Forum Building, Rm. 453
Harrisburg, PA 17120
(717) 787-5453 (specific questions)
(800) VISIT PA (847-4872) (travel literature)
Answers queries; distributes state visitors' guides, highway maps, and brochures

How to Use This Site Guide

The following site information guide will assist you in planning your tour of the natural areas of New Jersey, New York, and Pennsylvania. Sites set in boldface and followed by the symbol ❖ in the text are here organized alphabetically by state. Each entry is followed by the mailing address (sometimes different from the street address) and phone number of the immediate managing office, plus brief notes and a list of facilities and activities available. (A key appears on each page.)

Information on hours of operation, seasonal closings, and fees is often not listed, as these vary from season to season and year to year. Please bear in mind that responsibility for the management of some sites may change. Call well in advance to obtain maps, brochures, and pertinent, up-to-date information that will help you plan your adventures in the Mid-Atlantic region.

Each site entry in the guide includes the address and phone number of its immediate managing agency. Many of these sites are under the stewardship of a forest or park ranger or supervised from a small nearby office. Hence, in many cases, those sites will be difficult to contact directly, and it is preferable to call the managing agency.

The following umbrella organizations can provide general information for individual natural sites, as well as the area as a whole:

New Jersey
New Jersey Department of Environmental Protection
401 E. State St., 7th Fl.
CN 402
(609) 292-2885
(609) 292-9410
(Division of Fish, Game, and Wildlife)
(609) 984-0370 (Division of Parks and Forestry)

New York
Adirondack Park Agency
PO Box 99
Ray Brook, NY 12977
(518) 891-4050

New York State Department of Environmental Conservation
50 Wolf Rd.
Albany, NY 12233
(518) 457-3446
(518) 457-5690 (Division of Fish and Wildlife)
(518) 457-2475 (Division of Lands and Forests)

New York State Office of Parks, Recreation, and Historic Preservation
Empire State Plaza
Agency Bldg. 1
Albany, NY 12238
(518) 474-0456

Pennsylvania
Pennsylvania Department of Conservation and Natural Resources
PO Box 8767
Harrisburg, PA 17105
(717) 787-2869
(717) 787-2703 (Bureau of Forestry)
(717) 787-6640 (Bureau of State Parks)

Pennsylvania Game Commission
2001 Elmerton Ave.
Harrisburg, PA 17110
(717) 787-4250

Regional
National Park Service (NJ and PA)
Independence National Historical Park
313 Walnut St.
Philadelphia, PA 19106
(215) 597-8787

National Park Service (NY)
26 Wall St.
New York, NY 10005
(212) 264-8711

The Nature Conservancy
Eastern Regional Office
201 Devonshire St., 5th Fl.
Boston, MA 02110
(617) 542-1908

U.S. Fish and Wildlife Service
Northeast Regional Office
300 Westgate Center Dr.
Hadley, MA 01035
(413) 253-8200

U.S. Forest Service
310 W. Wisconsin Ave.
Rm. 500
Milwaukee, WI 53203
(414) 297-3600

267

NEW JERSEY

**ASSUNPINK WILDLIFE
MANAGEMENT AREA**
New Jersey Div. of Fish,
Game and Wildlife
386 Clarksburg-Robbinsville Rd.
Robbinsville, NJ 08691
(609) 259-2132　**BW, CK, F, H, HR, I, XC**

**BEARFORT MOUNTAIN
NATURAL AREA**
Wawayanda State Park
PO Box 198, Highland Park, NJ 07422
(201) 853-4462　**BW, F, H**

BELLEPLAIN STATE FOREST
New Jersey State Park Service
PO Box 450, Rte. 550
Woodbine, NJ 08270
(609) 861-2404　**BT, BW, C, CK, F, H, HR,
I, L, MB, MT, PA, S, T, TG, XC**

CAPE MAY BIRD OBSERVATORY
New Jersey Audubon Society
707 East Lake Dr., Box 3
Cape May, NJ 08212
(609) 884-2736
(609) 884-2626 (birding hotline)
　Check with office for scheduled events; facilities available at adjacent park　**BW, I**

CAPE MAY POINT STATE PARK
New Jersey State Park Service
PO Box 107, Cape May Point, NJ 08212
(609) 884-2159
　Tours and guides seasonally
BW, F, GS, H, I, MT, PA, T, TG

CEDAR SWAMP NATURAL AREA
New Jersey Div. of Parks and Forestry
PO Box 215, New Lisbon, NJ 08064
(609) 726-119　**BW, H, MB, MT, T**

**CHARLES H. ROGERS
WILDLIFE REFUGE**
Princeton Township
369 Witherspoon St., Princeton, NJ 08540
(609) 924-2271; (609) 924-5258
　Tours by prearrangement
BW, CK, F, H, TG

**DELAWARE WATER GAP
NATIONAL RECREATION AREA**
National Park Service
Bushkill, PA 18324
(717) 588-2451　**BW, C, CK, F, H, I, MT,
PA, RA, RC, S, T, XC**

**DENNIS CREEK WILDLIFE
MANAGEMENT AREA**
New Jersey Div. of Fish,
Game and Wildlife
CN 400, Trenton, NJ 08625-0400
(609) 292-9450　**BW, H**

DRYDEN-KUSER NATURAL AREA
High Point State Park
1480 Rte. 23, Sussex, NJ 07461
(201) 875-4800　**BW, MT, XC**

**EDWIN B. FORSYTHE NATIONAL
WILDLIFE REFUGE**
U.S. Fish and Wildlife Service
PO Box 72, Oceanville, NJ 08231
(609) 652-1665
　Entrance fee; wildlife drive; nature trails
BW, I, MT, T

**GREAT BAY BOULEVARD
WILDLIFE MANAGEMENT AREA**
New Jersey Div. of
Fish, Game and Wildlife
386 Clarksburg-Robbinsville Rd.
Robbinsville, NJ 08691
(609) 259-2132　**BW, F**

**GREAT EGG HARBOR NATIONAL SCENIC
AND RECREATIONAL RIVER**
National Park Service
200 Chestnut St.
Philadelphia, PA 19106
(609) 645-5960 (Atlantic County Parks
and Recreation)
　River flows through land primarily privately owned, access limited; facilities in parks
**BT, BW, C, CK, F, H, I,
L, PA, RA, S, T, TG, XC**

**GREAT SWAMP NATIONAL
WILDLIFE REFUGE**
U.S. Fish and Wildlife Service
RD 1, Box 152, Basking Ridge, NJ 07920
(201) 425-1222　**BW, H, MT, RA, T, XC**

**GREENWOOD FOREST
WILDLIFE MANAGEMENT AREA/
WEBBS MILL BOG**
New Jersey Div. of Fish, Game and Wildlife
386 Clarksburg-Robbinsville Rd.
Robbinsville, NJ 08691
(609) 259-2132　**BW, CK, F, H**

HAMILTON/TRENTON MARSH
Delaware and Raritan Greenway
570 Mercer Rd., Princeton, NJ 08540
(609) 924-4646　**BW, CK, F, H, MT, PA, TG**

BT	Bike Trails	**CK**	Canoeing, Kayaking	**F**	Fishing	**HR**	Horseback Riding
BW	Bird-watching			**GS**	Gift Shop		
C	Camping	**DS**	Downhill Skiing	**H**	Hiking	**I**	Information Center

HEMLOCK RAVINE NATURAL AREA
Wawayanda State Park
PO Box 198, Highland Lakes, NJ 07422
(201) 853-4462   **BW, F, H, HR, MB, XC**

**HIGBEE BEACH WILDLIFE
MANAGEMENT AREA**
New Jersey Div. of Fish, Game and Wildlife
2201 County Rte. 631
Woodbine, NJ 08270
(609) 628-2103   **BW, F, H, MT**

HIGH POINT STATE PARK
New Jersey State Park Service
1480 Rte. 23, Sussex, NJ 07461
(201) 825-4800
    **BT, BW, C, CK, F, H, HR, I,
MB, MT, PA, S, T, XC**

**HUBER WOODS PARK AND
ENVIRONMENTAL CENTER**
Monmouth County Parks System
805 Newman Springs Rd.
Lincroft, NJ 07738-1695
(908) 842-4000
(908) 872-2670   **BW, H, HR, I,
MB, MT, RA, T, XC**

INSTITUTE WOODS
Institute for Advanced Study
Olden Lane, Princeton, NJ 08540
(609) 734-8000   **BW**

ISLAND BEACH STATE PARK
New Jersey State Park Service
PO Box 37, Seaside Park, NJ 08752
(908) 793-0506
(908) 793-1698 (Aeolium Nature Center)
Disabled-accessible walkways to beach
and special surf chairs available for
beach access
    BW, CK, F, HR, MT, RA, S, T, XC

**KEN LOCKWOOD GORGE
WILDLIFE MANAGEMENT AREA**
New Jersey Div. of Fish,
Game and Wildlife
c/o Whittingham Wildlife
Management Area
150 Fredon-Springdale Rd.
Newton, NJ 07860
(201) 383-0918   **BT, BW, F**

LEBANON STATE FOREST
New Jersey State Forestry Service
PO Box 215, New Lisbon, NJ 08064
(609) 726-1191   **BT, BW, C, F, H, I,
MB, MT, PA, T**

LORD STIRLING PARK
Somerset County Park Commission
190 Lord Stirling Rd.
Basking Ridge, NJ 07920
(908) 766-2489   **BW, CK, F, GS, H, HR, I,
MT, RA, T, TG, XC**

**MAURICE NATIONAL
SCENIC AND RECREATIONAL RIVER**
National Park Service
200 Chestnut St.
Philadelphia, PA 19106
(609) 453-2177 (Cumberland County Dept.
of Planning and Development)
    BW, C, CK, F

MULLICA RIVER
Wharton State Forest
Batsto RD 9, Hammonton, NJ 08037
(609) 561-0024
(609) 268-0444 (Atsion Recreation Area)
    BW, CK

NUMMY ISLAND
Stone Harbor Chamber of Commerce
263 96th St., Stone Harbor, NJ 08247
(609) 368-6101   **BW**

OSWEGO RIVER NATURAL AREA
Wharton State Forest
Batsto RD 9
Hammonton, NJ 08037
(609) 561-0024
Information center at Batsto   **BW, CK, H, I**

PALISADES INTERSTATE PARK
Palisades Interstate Park Commission
PO Box 155
Alpine, NJ 07620-0155
(201) 768-1360   **BT, BW, CK, F, GS, H, I,
MT, PA, RA, T, XC**

PINE BARRENS
National Park Service
PO Box 118
Mauricetown, NJ 08329
(609) 785-0676
Much of area is private property
    **BT, BW, C, CK, F, GS, H,
HR, I, MB, MT, PA, S, T, TG**

**PYRAMID MOUNTAIN
NATURAL HISTORICAL AREA**
Morris County Park Commission
472A Boonton Ave.
Boonton, NJ 07005
(201) 334-3130
Visitor center open Friday–Sunday, 10
A.M. to 4 P.M.   **BW, H, I, MT, RA, T, TG**

L Lodging	**PA** Picnic Areas	**RC** Rock Climbing	**TG** Tours, Guides
MB Mountain Biking	**RA** Ranger-led Activities	**S** Swimming	**XC** Cross-country Skiing
MT Marked Trails		**T** Toilets	

REED'S BEACH
New Jersey Div. of Fish,
Game and Wildlife
2201 County Rte. 631, Woodbine, NJ 08270
(609) 628-2103
Most of area is private property; birding allowed in restricted area only **BW**

ROEBLING MEMORIAL PARK
Mercer County Park Commission
PO Box 8068, Trenton, NJ 08650-0068
(609) 989-6559 **BW, CK, F, H, MT, PA, TG**

SANDY HOOK
Gateway National Recreation Area
National Park Service
PO Box 530, Sandy Hook, NJ 07732
(908) 872-5970
Special-use fee for vehicles in summer;
nighttime fishing requires permit; camping for organized youth groups only
BW, CK, F, GS, H, I, MT, PA, RA, S, T, TG

SEDGE ISLAND
Stone Harbor Chamber of Commerce
263 96th St., Stone Harbor, NJ 08247
(609) 368-6101 **BW**

STOKES STATE FOREST
New Jersey State Park Service
1 Coursen Rd., Branchville, NJ 07826
(201) 948-3820
Maps and regulations available at office
**BW, C, F, H, HR, I, MB,
MT, PA, S, T, XC**

TROY MEADOWS
Ringwood State Park
1304 Sloatsburg Rd.
Ringwood, NJ 07456
(201) 962-7031 **BW, H**

**WALLKILL RIVER
NATIONAL WILDLIFE REFUGE**
U.S. Fish and Wildlife Service
PO Box 383, Sussex, NJ 07461
(201) 702-7266
Contact refuge for information on which
areas are open to public
BW, F, H, I, MT, XC

WAWAYANDA STATE PARK
New Jersey State Park Service
PO Box 198, Highland Lakes, NJ 07422
(201) 853-4462
Parking fee in summer
**BT, BW, C, CK, F, H, HR, I,
MB, MT, PA, S, T, XC**

**WAWAYANDA SWAMP
NATURAL AREA**
Wawayanda State Park
PO Box 198
Highland Lakes, NJ 07422
(201) 853-4462 **BT, BW, C, F,
H, HR, MB, MT, XC**

WEST PINE PLAINS NATURAL AREA
Bass River State Forest
PO Box 118, Stage Rd.
New Gretna, NJ 08094
(609) 296-1114 **BW, H, HR**

WHARTON STATE FOREST
New Jersey State Park Service
Batsto RD 9, Hammonton, NJ 08037
(609) 561-0024
(609) 268-0444 (Atsion Recreation Area)
Swimming at recreation center only
**BW, C, CK, F, GS, H, HR, I,
MB, MT, PA, S, T, TG**

**WILLIAM D. AND JUNE C. BLAIR CAPE
MAY MIGRATORY BIRD REFUGE**
The Nature Conservancy
200 Pottersville Rd., Chester, NJ 07930
(908) 879-7262
Observation platform **BW, MT, TG**

NEW YORK

ADIRONDACK PARK
Adirondack Park Agency
Visitor Interpretive Center,
Box 3000
Paul Smiths, NY 12983
(518) 327-3000
**BT, BW, C, CK, DS, F, H, HR, I, L, MB,
MT, PA, RA, RC, S, T, TG, XC**

ALLEGANY STATE PARK
New York State Office of Parks,
Recreation and Historic
Preservation
Western District, Allegany Region
2373 ASP Rte. 1, Ste. 3
Salamanca, NY 14779
(716) 354-9101 **BT, BW, C, CK, F, GS, H,
HR, I, L, MB, MT, PA, RA, S, T, TG, XC**

AUSABLE CHASM
PO Box 390, Rte. 9
Ausable Chasm, NY 12911
(518) 834-7454
Open Memorial Day through Columbus
Day; admission fee **C, GS, I, L,
PA, T, TG, XC**

BT	Bike Trails	**CK**	Canoeing, Kayaking	**F**	Fishing	**HR**	Horseback Riding
BW	Bird-watching			**GS**	Gift Shop		
C	Camping	**DS**	Downhill Skiing	**H**	Hiking	**I**	Information Center

BEAR MOUNTAIN STATE PARK
Palisades Interstate Park Commission
Administration Bldg.
Bear Mountain, NY 10911
(914) 786-2701, ext. 270 (visitor services);
ext. 263 (trailside museums and zoo)
Tours by prearrangement
BT, BW, C, CK, F, GS, H, HR, I,
L, MT, PA, RA, S, T, TG, XC

BUTTERMILK FALLS STATE PARK
New York State Office of Parks,
Recreation and Historic Preservation
Finger Lakes Region
RD 10, Ithaca, NY 14850
(607) 273-5761
Cabins available BW, C, F, H, L, MT, PA,
RA, S, T, TG, XC

CATSKILL PARK
New York Bureau of
Preserve Protection and Management
50 Wolf Rd., Rm. 438
Albany, NY 12233-4255
(518) 457-7433
Includes Catskill Forest Preserve
BT, BW, C, DS, F, H,
HR, MB, MT, PA, RC, S, XC

CENTRAL PARK
City of New York Parks and
Recreation Dept.
Central Park Conservancy
The Arsenal, Central Park
New York, NY 10021
(212) 360-3444
Catch-and-release fishing at Charles A.
Dana Discovery Center; inquire about
tours at The Dairy BW, F, H, HR, I,
PA, RA, S, T, TG, XC

CHIMNEY BLUFFS STATE PARK
New York State Office
of Parks, Recreation and
Historic Preservation
Finger Lakes Region
c/o Fair Haven Beach State Park
Rte. 104A
Fair Haven, NY 13064 BW, F, H

CHITTENANGO FALLS STATE PARK
New York State Office of
Parks, Recreation and
Historic Preservation
Central Region
6105 East Seneca Turnpike
Jamesville, NY 13078-9516
(315) 655-9620 BW, C, H, PA, T

CLARK RESERVATION
New York State Office of Parks, Recreation
and Historic Preservation, Central Region
6105 East Seneca Turnpike
Jamesville, NY 13078-9516
(315) 492-1590
Information center open seasonally
BW, F, H, I, PA, T, TG

**CONNETQUOT RIVER
STATE PARK PRESERVE**
New York State Office of Parks, Recreation
and Historic Preservation
Long Island Region
PO Box 247, Babylon, NY 11702
(516) 669-1000 (headquarters)
(516) 581-1005 (preserve)
Visitor permit required; fly-fishing by
reservation only BW, F, H, HR,
I, MT, RA, T, TG, XC

CRANBERRY BOG COUNTY PRESERVE
Suffolk County Dept. of Parks, Recreation
and Conservation
PO Box 144, Montauk Hwy.
West Sayville, NY 11796
(516) 854-4949
Call office for entry pass BW, H, MT

DAVID WELD SANCTUARY
The Nature Conservancy
Long Island Chapter
250 Lawrence Hill Rd.
Cold Spring Harbor, NY 11724
(516) 367-3225
No pets; foot traffic only; no collecting
BW, H, I, MT

DERBY HILL BIRD OBSERVATORY
Onondaga Audubon Society
PO Box 620, Syracuse, NY 13201
(315) 457-7731 (year-round)
(315) 963-8291 (March to May)
Blind provided for marsh viewing
BW, H, MT, PA, T, XC

EL DORADO BEACH PRESERVE
The Nature Conservancy
315 Alexander St., Ste. 301
Rochester, NY 14604
(716) 546-8030
Controlled access; stay on trails; follow
posted regulations BW, H, MT

FILLMORE GLEN STATE PARK
New York State Office of Parks, Recreation
and Historic Preservation
Finger Lakes Region

L Lodging	**PA** Picnic Areas	**RC** Rock Climbing	**TG** Tours, Guides
MB Mountain Biking	**RA** Ranger-led Activities	**S** Swimming	**XC** Cross-country Skiing
MT Marked Trails		**T** Toilets	

271

RD 3, Box 26, Moravia, NY 13118
(315) 497-0130
Cabins available   **BW, C, F, H, L, MT, PA, RA, S, T, TG, XC**

FIRE ISLAND NATIONAL SEASHORE
National Park Service
120 Laurel St., Patchogue, NY 11772
(516) 289-4810
Some facilities available summer only
BW, C, CK, F, GS, H, I, MT, RA, S, T

FIVE PONDS WILDERNESS
Adirondack Park
Visitor Interpretive Center, Box 3000
Paul Smiths, NY 12983
(518) 327-3000
Check with office for possible trail closures
BW, C, CK, F, H, MB, L, MT, PA, S, XC

GADWAY SANDSTONE PAVEMENT BARRENS PRESERVE
The Nature Conservancy
Adirondack Chapter
PO Box 65, Keene Valley, NY 12943
(518) 576-2082   **BW, H, XC**

GREEN LAKES STATE PARK
New York State Office of Parks, Recreation
and Historic Preservation, Central Region
6105 East Seneca Turnpike
Jamesville, NY 13078-9516
(315) 637-6111   **BW, C, F, H, PA, S, T, TG, XC**

HARRIMAN STATE PARK
Palisades Interstate Park Commission
Administration Bldg.
Bear Mountain, NY 10911
(914) 786-2701, ext. 270
Parking and entry fees
BT, BW, C, F, GS, H, HR, I, L, MB, MT, PA, RA, RC, S, T, TG, XC

HIGH FALLS GORGE
Roanka Attractions
Rte. 86 at Wilmington Notch
Wilmington, NY 12997
(518) 946-2278
Fee for self-guided tours
BW, F, GS, H, MT, T, TG

ICE CAVES MOUNTAIN
PO Box 430
Walker Valley, NY 12588
(914) 647-7989
Open May–October; admission fee; self-
guided tours   **GS, I, T, TG**

IROQUOIS NATIONAL WILDLIFE REFUGE
U.S. Fish and Wildlife Service
PO Box 51, Alabama, NY 14003-0517
(716) 948-5445   **BT, BW, CK, F, H, I, RA, T, TG, XC**

ITHACA FALLS
City of Ithaca
108 East Green St., Ithaca, NY 14850
(607) 274-6570   **PA**

JAMAICA BAY WILDLIFE REFUGE
Gateway National Recreation Area
National Park Service
Floyd Bennett Field
Brooklyn, NY 11234
(718) 318-4340   **BW, F, GS, H, I, MT, RA, T, TG**

JOHN BOYD THACHER STATE PARK
New York State Office of Parks, Recreation
and Historic Preservation
Saratoga Capital District Region
RD 1, Box 238
Vorheesville, NY 12186
(518) 872-1237   **BT, BW, GS, H, I, MB, MT, PA, RA, S, T, TG, XC**

LABRADOR HOLLOW STATE NATURE PRESERVE
New York State Div. of Lands and Forests
1285 Fisher Ave., Cortland, NY 13045-1090
(607) 753-3095
Group tours by prearrangement
BW, CK, F, H, MT, T, TG, XC

LAKE CHAMPLAIN
Adirondack Park Agency
Visitor Interpretive Center, Box 3000
Paul Smiths, NY 12983
(518) 327-3000   **BW, C, CK, F, H, I, MT, MT, PA, S, T**

LAKE GEORGE
Adirondack Park Agency
Visitor Interpretive Center, Box 3000
Paul Smiths, NY 12983
(518) 327-3000
BW, C, CK, F, H, I, MT, PA, S, T

LAKEVIEW WILDLIFE MANAGEMENT AREA
New York State Dept. of Environmental
Conservation
317 Washington St.
Watertown, NY 13601
(315) 785-2261; (315) 639-6122
Best views from canoes
BW, CK, F, H, MT, T, XC

BT Bike Trails	**CK** Canoeing, Kayaking	**F** Fishing	**HR** Horseback Riding
BW Bird-watching		**GS** Gift Shop	
C Camping	**DS** Downhill Skiing	**H** Hiking	**I** Information Center

LETCHWORTH STATE PARK
New York State Office of Parks, Recreation
and Historic Preservation
Western District, Genesee Region, 1 LSP
Castile, NY 14427
(716) 493-3600
Cabins available   **BT, BW, C, CK, F, GS,
H, HR, I, L, MB, MT, PA, RA, S, T, TG, XC**

MASHOMACK PRESERVE
The Nature Conservancy
PO Box 850
Shelter Island, NY 11964
(516) 749-1001   **BW, GS, H, I, MT, TG**

MENDON PONDS COUNTY PARK
County of Monroe, Parks Dept.
171 Reservoir Ave., Rochester, NY 14620
(716) 256-4950   **BW, CK, F, GS, H, HR,
MT, PA, T, TG, XC**

**MIANUS RIVER GORGE WILDLIFE
REFUGE AND BOTANICAL PRESERVE**
Mianus River Gorge Preserve, Inc.
167 Mianus River Rd., Bedford, NY 10506
(914) 234-3455
Closed to public December 1 to April 1
BW, H, MT

**MINNA ANTHONY COMMON
NATURE CENTER**
Wellesley Island State Park
PO Box 247, Alexandria Bay, NY 13607
(315) 482-2479; (315) 482-2722
**BW, C, CK, F, GS, H, I,
MT, PA, RA, S, T, TG, XC**

MINNEWASKA STATE PARK PRESERVE
Palisades Interstate Park Commission
PO Box 893, New Paltz, NY 12561
(914) 255-0752   **BT, BW, H, HR, I, MT,
PA, RA, S, T, XC**

MOHONK PRESERVE
1000 Mountain Rest Rd.
New Paltz, NY 12561
(914) 255-0919
Mountain biking and rock climbing by
permit in designated areas
**BW, GS, H, HR, I,
MB, MT, RA, RC, TG, XC**

MONTAUK COUNTY PARK
Suffolk County Dept. of Parks,
Recreation and Conservation
PO Box 144, Montauk Hwy.
West Sayville, NY 11796
(516) 854-4949 **BW, C, F, H, HR, MT, PA, T**

MONTAUK POINT STATE PARK
New York State Office of Parks, Recreation
and Historic Preservation
Long Island Region
RR 2, Box 206A, South Fairview Ave.
Montauk, NY 11954
(516) 668-3781   **BW, F, GS, H, HR, PA, T**

**MONTEZUMA NATIONAL
WILDLIFE REFUGE**
U.S. Fish and Wildlife Service
3395 Rtes. 5/20 East
Seneca Falls, NY 13148
(315) 568-5987
Observation towers with telescopes
BW, I, MT, T

**MORTON NATIONAL
WILDLIFE REFUGE**
U.S. Fish and Wildlife Service
Long Island National Wildlife
Refuge Complex
PO Box 21, Shirley, NY 11967
(516) 286-0485   **BW, F, H, MT, T**

NIAGARA RESERVATION STATE PARK
New York State Office of Parks, Recreation
and Historic Preservation
Western District, Niagara Region
PO Box 1132
Niagara Falls, NY 14303-0132
(716) 278-1770
(716) 278-1796 (Orin Lehman Park
Visitor Center)
(716) 278-1730 (Cave of the Winds)
(716) 278-1780 (Schoellkopf
Geological Museum)
(716) 284-4233 (Maid of the Mist boat trip)
BW, F, GS, I, PA, RA, T, TG

**OAK ORCHARD WILDLIFE
MANAGEMENT AREA**
New York State Dept. of Environmental
Conservation
PO Box 422
Alabama, NY 14003-0422
(716) 948-5182
BT, BW, CK, F, H, HR, MB, XC

ROBERT H. TREMAN STATE PARK
New York State Office of
Parks, Recreation and
Historic Preservation
Finger Lakes Region
RD 10, Ithaca, NY 14850
(607) 273-3440
Cabins available
BW, C, F, H, L, MT, PA, RA, S, T, TG

L	Lodging	**PA**	Picnic Areas	**RC**	Rock Climbing	**TG**	Tours, Guides
MB	Mountain Biking	**RA**	Ranger-led Activities	**S**	Swimming	**XC**	Cross-country Skiing
MT	Marked Trails			**T**	Toilets		

273

ROCK CITY
505 Rock City Rd., Olean, NY 14760
(716) 373-7790
  Admission fee; allow minimum of one
  hour; open May–October
                        GS, H, I, MT, PA, T, TG

SHEQUAGA FALLS
Village of Montour Falls
PO Box 812, Montour Falls, NY 14865
(607) 535-7367   **PA**

SOUTHWICK BEACH STATE PARK
New York State Office of Parks, Recreation
and Historic Preservation
Thousand Islands Regions
PO Box 247
Alexandria Bay, NY 13607
(315) 938-5083 (winter)
(315) 846-5338 (summer)
            BW, C, H, I, MT, PA, RA, S, T, XC

TAUGHANNOCK FALLS STATE PARK
New York State Office of Parks, Recreation
and Historic Preservation
Finger Lakes Region
PO Box 1055, Trumansburg, NY 14886
(617) 387-6739
  Cabins available; trail to falls negotiable
  by wheelchairs with assistance
                       BW, C, F, H, L, MT,
                       PA, RA, S, T, TG, XC

THOUSAND ISLANDS
New York State Office of Parks,
Recreation and Historic Preservation
Thousand Islands Region
PO Box 247
Alexandria Bay, NY 13607
(315) 482-2593   **BW, C, CK, F, GS, H, I,**
                     MT, PA, RA, S, T, TG, XC

TONAWANDA WILDLIFE
MANAGEMENT AREA
New York State Dept. of
Environmental Conservation
PO Box 422
Alabama, NY 14003-0422
(716) 948-5182   **BT, BW, CK, F, H, HR,**
                           MB, XC

UPPER HUDSON RIVER GORGE
Adirondack Park Agency
Visitor Interpretive Center, Box 3000
Paul Smiths, NY 12983
(518) 327-3000
  For experienced boaters only
            BW, CK, F, H, MT, S, T, TG

WATKINS GLEN STATE PARK
New York State Office of Parks,
Recreation and Historic Preservation
Finger Lakes Region
PO Box 304, Watkins Glen, NY 14891
(607) 535-4511   **BW, C, F, GS, H, L, MT,**
                           PA, RA, S, T, TG, XC

WELLESLEY ISLAND STATE PARK
New York State Office
of Parks, Recreation and Historic
Preservation
Thousand Islands Region
PO Box 247, Alexandria Bay, NY 13607
(315) 482-2722
(315) 482-2593   **BW, C, CK, F, GS, H,**
                           I, MT, PA, RA, S, T, TG, XC

WHETSTONE GULF STATE PARK
New York State Office of Parks, Recreation
and Historic Preservation
Thousand Islands Region
PO Box 247, Alexandria Bay, NY 13607
(315) 376-6630; (315) 482-2593
            BW, C, CK, F, H, I, MT, PA, S, T, XC

WHIRLPOOL STATE PARK
New York State Office of Parks, Recreation
and Historic Preservation, Niagara Region
PO Box 1132, Niagara Falls, NY 14303-0132
(716) 278-1770
  Scenic overlook   **BW, H, MT, PA, T**

WHITEFACE MOUNTAIN
Adirondack Park Agency
Visitor Interpretive Center, Box 3000
Paul Smiths, NY 12983
(518) 327-3000
  Road admission fee   **BW, H, I, MT, PA, T**

PENNSYLVANIA

ALLEGHENY NATIONAL FOREST
U.S. Forest Service
222 Liberty St., Warren, PA 16365
(814) 723-5150; (814) 726-2710 (TTY)
                   BT, BW, C, CK, F, GS,
                   H, HR, I, MB, MT, PA, S, T

ARCHBALD POTHOLE STATE PARK
Lackawanna State Park
RR 1, Box 230, Dalton, PA 18414
(717) 945-3239   **BW, H, MT, PA, T**

BARTRAM'S GARDEN
54th St. and Lindbergh Blvd.
Philadelphia, PA 19143
(215) 729-5281
                   BT, BW, GS, I, MT, PA, T, TG

BT Bike Trails	**CK** Canoeing, Kayaking	**F** Fishing	**HR** Horseback Riding
BW Bird-watching		**GS** Gift Shop	
C Camping	**DS** Downhill Skiing	**H** Hiking	**I** Information Center

BEAR MEADOWS NATURAL AREA
Rothrock State Forest
PO Box 403, Rothrock Lane
Huntington, PA 16652
(814) 643-2340   **BW, H, MT**

BEAR RUN NATURE RESERVE
Western Pennsylvania Conservancy
316 Fourth Ave., Pittsburgh, PA 15222-2075
(412) 288-2777   **BW, C, H, MT, XC**

**BOWMAN'S HILL
WILDFLOWER PRESERVE**
Pennsylvania Historic and
Museum Commission
PO Box 685, New Hope, PA 18938-0685
(215) 862-2924   **BW, GS, I, MT, RA, T, TG**

BRISTOL MARSH
The Nature Conservancy
1211 Chestnut St.
Philadelphia, PA 19107
(215) 963-1400   **BW, F, H, MT**

BUCKTAIL STATE PARK NATURAL AREA
Little Pine State Park Complex
HC 63, Box 100
Waterville, PA 17776-9705
(717) 753-6000; (814) 486-3365
           BW, CK, F, H

BUSHKILL FALLS
Bushkill Falls Rd., Bushkill, PA 18324
(717) 588-6682
   Admission fee   **BW, F, GS, H, I, MT, PA, T**

COLTON POINT STATE PARK
c/o Leonard Harrison State Park
RD 6, Box 199, Wellsboro, PA 16901
(717) 724-3061
       BT, BW, C, F, H, MT, PA, T, XC

COOK FOREST STATE PARK
Pennsylvania Bureau of State Parks
PO Box 120, Cooksburg, PA 16217
(814) 744-8407
   Cabins available; tours and guides summer only   **BW, C, CK, F, H, HR, I, L, MT, PA, RA, S, T, TG, XC**

DANIEL BOONE HOMESTEAD
Pennsylvania Historical and
Museum Commission
400 Daniel Boone Rd.
Birdsboro, PA 19508
(610) 582-4900
   Camping for organized youth groups only
     BW, F, GS, H, HR, I, MT, PA, RA, T, TG

DAVID M. RODERICK WILDLIFE RESERVE
(State Game Lands No. 314)
Pennsylvania Game Commission
2001 Elmerton, PA 17110-9797
(814) 432-3187   **BW, F, H, HR, MB, XC**

**DELAWARE WATER GAP NATIONAL
RECREATION AREA**
National Park Service
Bushkill, PA 18324
(717) 588-2451   **BW, C, CK, F, H, I, MT, PA, RA, RC, S, T, XC**

DELHAAS WOODS
Silver Lake Nature Center
Bucks County Dept. of
Parks and Recreation
1306 Bath Rd.
Bristol, PA 19007
(215) 785-1177   **BW, F, GS, H, I, PA, RA, T, TG**

DINGMANS FALLS VISITOR CENTER
Delaware Water Gap
National Recreation Area
National Park Service
Bushkill, PA 18324
(717) 828-7802; (717) 588-2451
       GS, I, MT, PA, RA, T, TG

**EDWARD WOOLMAN
NATURE PRESERVE**
The Nature Conservancy
1200 Chestnut St., Philadelphia, PA 19107
(215) 963-1400   **BW, H**

ELK STATE FOREST
Pennsylvania Bureau of Forestry
PO Box 327, Emporium, PA 15834
(814) 486-335   **BW, C, F, H, HR, MB, MT, PA, XC**

ENLOW FORK NATURAL AREA
(State Game Lands No. 302)
Pennsylvania Game Commission
2001 Elmerton, PA 17110-9797
(412) 238-9523   **BW, F, H, HR, MB, XC**

ERIE NATIONAL WILDLIFE REFUGE
U.S. Fish and Wildlife Service
11296 Wood Duck Lane
Guys Mills, PA 16327
(814) 789-3585   **BW, CK, F, H, I, MT, PA, T, TG, XC**

FERNCLIFF PENINSULA
Ohiopyle State Park
PO Box 105, Ohiopyle, PA 15470
(412) 329-8591   **BW, H, MT, RA**

L Lodging	**PA** Picnic Areas	**RC** Rock Climbing	**TG** Tours, Guides
MB Mountain Biking	**RA** Ranger-led Activities	**S** Swimming	**XC** Cross-country Skiing
MT Marked Trails		**T** Toilets	

275

FLORENCE SHELLY PRESERVE
The Nature Conservancy
1211 Chestnut St., Philadelphia, PA 19107
(215) 963-1400 (TNC)
(717) 756-2429 (preserve)   **BW, H, MT, TG**

GEORGE W. CHILD RECREATION SITE
Delaware Water Gap
National Recreation Area
National Park Service
Bushkill, PA 18324
(717) 588-2451   **BW, H, MT, PA, T**

HAWK MOUNTAIN SANCTUARY
RR 2, Box 191, Kempton, PA 19529
(610) 756-6961   **BW, GS, H, MT, RA, T**

HAYSTACKS OF LOYALSOCK CREEK
Pennsylvania Bureau of Forestry
RR 2, Box 47, Bloomsburg, PA 17815
(717) 387-4255; (717) 924-3501
Hike to haystacks three miles round-trip
BW, H, MT

HEARTS CONTENT SCENIC AREA
Allegheny National Forest
222 Liberty St., Warren, PA 16365
(814) 723-5150
Mountain biking on forest roads only;
primitive camping   **BW, C, F, H, HR, L,
MB, MT, PA, T, XC**

HICKORY CREEK WILDERNESS AREA
Allegheny National Forest
222 Liberty St., Warren, PA 16365
(814) 723-5150
Primitive camping   **BW, C, F, H, HR,
MT, PA, T, T, XC**

HICKORY RUN STATE PARK
Pennsylvania Bureau of State Parks
RD 1, Box 81, White Haven, PA 18661
(717) 443-0400   **BW, C, F, H, I, MT,
PA, RA, S, T, XC**

**HOVERTER AND SCHOLL BOX HUCKLE-
BERRY NATURAL AREA**
Pennsylvania Bureau of Forestry
District #3, RD 1, Box 42-A
Blain, PA 17006
(717) 536-3191   **BW, H, MT**

**HYNER RUN AND HYNER
VIEW STATE PARKS**
Little Pine State Park Complex
HC 63, Box 100
Waterville, PA 17776-9705
(717) 753-753-6000   **BW, CK, F, H**

**JENNINGS ENVIRONMENTAL
EDUCATION CENTER**
Pennsylvania Bureau of State Parks
2951 Prospect Rd.
Slippery Rock, PA 16057-8701
(412) 794-6011   **BW, H, I, MT,
PA, T, TG, XC**

JOHN HEINZ NATIONAL WILDLIFE REFUGE
U.S. Fish and Wildlife Service
International Plaza II, Suite 104
Philadelphia, PA 19113
(215) 365-3118   **BT, BW, CK, F, H, I, T, TG**

**KINGS GAP ENVIRONMENTAL EDUCATION
AND TRAINING CENTER**
Pennsylvania Bureau of State Parks
500 Kings Gap Rd., Carlisle, PA 17013
(717) 486-5031   **BW, H, I, MT, T**

LACAWAC SANCTUARY
RR 1, Box 518, Lake Ariel, PA 18436
(717) 689-9494
Nature trail open to public year-round;
access to lake and other areas by guided
tour only   **BW, GS, H, I, MT, TG**

LAUREL HIGHLANDS HIKING TRAIL
Laurel Ridge State Park
RD 3, Box 246, Rockwood, PA 15557
(412) 455-3744
Eight camping areas; no bicycles
BW, C, H, MT, PA

LEONARD HARRISON STATE PARK
Pennsylvania Bureau of State Parks
RD 6, Box 199, Wellsboro, PA 16901
(717) 724-3061
BW, C, F, H, I, MT, PA, RA, T

LOST RIVER CAVERNS
726 Durham St., PO Box M
Hellertown, PA 18055
(610) 838-8767
Admission fee   **GS, I, PA, T, TG**

MCCONNELL'S MILL STATE PARK
Pennsylvania Bureau of State Parks
RD 2, Box 16, Portersville, PA 16051
(412) 368-8091
(412) 368-9320 (Grist Mill, seasonal)
BW, CK, F, H, MT, PA, RC, T, TG

**MILL GROVE, THE AUDUBON
WILDLIFE SANCTUARY**
County of Montgomery
PO Box 7125, Audubon, PA 19407-7125
(610) 666-5593   **BW,GS, I, MT, T, TG, XC**

BT	Bike Trails	**CK**	Canoeing,	**F**	Fishing	**HR**	Horseback
BW	Bird-watching		Kayaking	**GS**	Gift Shop		Riding
C	Camping	**DS**	Downhill Skiing	**H**	Hiking	**I**	Information Center

MORAINE STATE PARK
Pennsylvania Bureau of State Parks
225 Pleasant Valley Rd.
Portersville, PA 16051
(412) 368-8811
Cabins available **BT, BW, CK, F, H, HR, I, L, MB, MT, PA, RA, S, T, XC**

MOUNT DAVIS NATURAL AREA
Forbes State Forest
PO Box 519, Laughlintown, PA 15655
(412) 238-9533 **BW, H, MT**

NOTTINGHAM COUNTY PARK
Pennsylvania Bureau of State Parks
Government Services Center, Ste. 160
601 Westtown Rd.
West Chester, PA 19382-4534
(610) 344-6415 **BW, C, F, H, HR, I, MT, PA, RA, RC, T, TG, XC**

OHIOPYLE STATE PARK
Pennsylvania Bureau of State Parks
PO Box 105, Ohiopyle, PA 15470
(412) 329-8591 **BT, BW, C, CK, F, GS, H, I, MB, MT, PA, RA, T, XC**

PINE CREEK GORGE
Pennsylvania Bureau of Forestry
Box 94, Rte. 287S, Wellsboro, PA 16901
(717) 724-2868 **BT, BW, CK, F, H, HR, MB, MT, PA**

PRESQUE ISLE STATE PARK
Pennsylvania Bureau of State Parks
PO Box 8510, Erie, PA 16505
(814) 871-4251
Check with office about restrictions in certain areas **BT, BW, CK, F, GS, H, I, MT, PA, RA, S, T, XC**

RACCOON CREEK STATE PARK
Pennsylvania Bureau of State Parks
3000 SR 18, Hookstown, PA 15050
(412) 899-2200
(412) 899-3611 (nature center) **BT, BW, C, CK, F, H, HR, I, L, MT, PA, S, T, TG, XC**

RICKETTS GLEN STATE PARK
Pennsylvania Bureau of State Parks
RD 2, Box 130, Benton, PA 17814-8905
(717) 477-5675
Cabins available **BW, C, CK, F, H, HR, I, L, MT, PA, RA, S, T, XC**

RINGING ROCKS COUNTY PARK
Bucks County Dept. of Parks
and Recreation

901 East Bridgetown Pike
Langhorne, PA 19047
(215) 757-0571 **BW, MT, T**

SEVEN TUBS NATURAL AREA
Luzerne County Parks Dept.
Moon Lake Park
RR 2, Box 301, Hunlock Creek, PA 18621
(717) 477-5467; (717) 256-3212
Day use only; open Memorial Day to
Labor Day **BW, MT, PA, T**

SHENK'S FERRY WILDFLOWER PRESERVE
Pennsylvania Power and Light Company
9 New Village Rd., Holtwood, PA 17532
(717) 284-2278
No flower picking; no horses; no bikes **BW, CK, H, MT, TG**

TANNERSVILLE CRANBERRY BOG
The Nature Conservancy
Monroe County Conservation District
8050 Running Valley Rd.
Stroudsburg, PA 18360
(717) 629-3061
Limited to guided access in some areas
of property **BW, H, MT, TG**

TROUGH CREEK STATE PARK
Pennsylvania Bureau of State Parks
RR 1, Box 211, James Creek, PA 16657-9302
(814) 658-3847 **BW, C, F, H, L, MT, PA, T**

TUCQUAN GLEN
Lancaster County Conservancy
PO Box 716, Lancaster, PA 17608-0716
(717) 392-7891 **BW, F, H**

WASHINGTON CROSSING HISTORIC PARK
Pennsylvania Historical and
Museum Commission
PO Box 103
Washington Crossing, PA 18977
(215) 493-4076
Seasonal interpretative programs; fees
for tours **BW, GS, I, T, TG**

WOLF CREEK NARROWS NATURAL AREA
Western Pennsylvania Conservancy
316 Fourth Ave.
Pittsburgh, PA 15222-2075
(412) 288-2777 **BW, F, H, MT**

**WOODBOURNE FOREST AND
WILDLIFE SANCTUARY**
The Nature Conservancy
1211 Chestnut St., Philadelphia, PA 19107
(215) 963-1400 **BW, H, MT, PA, RA, TG, XC**

L	Lodging	**PA**	Picnic Areas	**RC**	Rock Climbing
MB	Mountain Biking	**RA**	Ranger-led Activities	**S**	Swimming
MT	Marked Trails			**T**	Toilets

TG	Tours, Guides
XC	Cross-country Skiing

INDEX

ACKNOWLEDGMENTS

The editors gratefully acknowledge the professional assistance of Tish Fila, Susan Kirby, Phil Koslow, and Patricia Woodruff. We wish to thank those site managers and naturalists whose time and commitment contributed to this volume. The following consultants also helped in the preparation of this volume: Obediah B. Derr; Dr. David E. Fairbrothers, Professor of Botany (Emeritus), Rutgers University; Tony Ingraham, regional coordinator of environmental interpretation and recreation for the Finger Lakes Region of New York State Parks; Charles Johnson, State Naturalist, Agency of Natural Resources, Vermont Department of Forests, Parks, and Recreation; and Dallas Rhodes, Professor and Chair of Geology, Whittier College.

Among the dozens of people who shared their expertise to make this book possible, the author is especially grateful to the following: Scott Anderson of the New York Nature Conservancy; Jerry Book; Bob Cartica of the New Jersey Department of Environmental Protection and Energy; Michael Catania and Elizabeth Johnson of the Nature Conservancy's New Jersey chapter; Ad Crable of the *Lancaster New Era*; Dan Cusick of the *Scranton Times*; Pete Dunne, Paul Kerlinger, and Louise Zemaitis of New Jersey Audubon's Cape May Bird Observatory; Paul Huth of the Mohonk Preserve; Lance Martin and Jim Wilson of Wilderness Voyageurs; Deborah Mayer and Bud Cook of the Nature Conservancy's Pennsylvania chapter; Kathy Regan of the Adirondack Nature Conservancy; Jean Stull; Paul Wiegman of the Western Pennsylvania Conservancy; Martha Wolfe of Bartram's Garden.

PHOTOGRAPHY CREDITS

All photography by Jonathan Wallen except for the following:

i: Carl R. Sams II, Milford, MI
viii, right: Millard H. Sharp, Jacksonville, FL
xiii: John Hendrickson, Clipper Mills, CA
6–7: National Gallery of Art, Smithsonian Institution, Washington, D.C., Gift of the Avalon Foundation, 1963
8: Mike Barlow/Dembinsky Photo Associates (DPA), Owosso, MI
16: New York Public Library, Astor, Lenox and Tilden Foundations, New York, NY
18, 19, top,19, bottom right: Arthur Morris/Birds As Art, Deltona, FL
19, bottom left: Robert Villani, Merrick, NY
22: Bates Littlehales, Arlington, VA
23: Arthur Morris/Birds As Art

25: Collection of the New-York Historical Society, New York, NY
32: Leonard Lee Rue III, Blairstown, NJ
36, left: Arthur Morris/Birds As Art
38–39: The Minneapolis Institute of Arts, Minneapolis, MN
41: Tom Bean, Flagstaff, AZ
42: Library of Congress, Washington, D.C.
53: Robert Lankinen/The Wildlife Collection, Brooklyn, NY
57: Bates Littlehales
60: Tom and Pat Leeson, Vancouver, WA
61: Robert Villani
67: Courtesy of Seward House, Auburn, NY
78: Arthur Morris/Birds As Art
86: Courtesy of the Fogg Art Museum, Harvard University Art Museums,

Bequest of Grenville L. Winthrop, Cambridge, MA (#1943.304)
88, left: John Shaw, Colorado Springs, CO
88, right: Rod Planck/DPA
89: Carl R. Sams II/DPA
92: Jim Battles/DPA
94: Rod Planck/DPA
97: Paul Rezendes, South Royalston, MA
102: Michael S. Quinton, Slana, AK
105: John Hendrickson
120: American Philosophical Society, Philadelphia, PA
124: Collection of the New-York Historical Society
128, top: Arthur Morris/Birds As Art
128, bottom left: Robert Lankinen/ The Wildlife Collection
128, bottom right: John Mielcarek/DPA
140, 146: Leonard Lee Rue III
162, top: John Mielcarek/DPA
168, top left: Courtesy of Jennings Environmental Education Center, Slippery Rock, PA
176, left: Bates Littlehales
176, right: Arthur Morris/Birds As Art
177, left: Barbara Gerlach, Chatham, MI
177, right: Arthur Morris/Birds As Art
181: The Detroit Institute of Arts, Gift of Dexter M. Ferry, Jr.
184: Paul Rezendes
195: Arthur Morris/Birds As Art
196: Dr. Scott Nielsen, Superior, WI
203, right: John Hendrickson
206, left: Dr. Scott Nielsen
210: John Shaw
214: Bates Littlehales
222: Arthur Morris/Birds As Art
227: A.B. Sheldon/DPA
230, left: John Gerlach/DPA
236: Arthur Morris/Birds As Art
238: Millard H. Sharp
242, left: Robert Villani
242, right, 243, top, 243, bottom right: Arthur Morris/Birds As Art
243, bottom left: Harold Lindstrom, Baiting Hollow, NY
245: Paul Rezendes
258–59: Glenn D. Chambers, Columbia, MO
261: Courtesy of the Adirondack Museum, Blue Lake Mountain, NY
263: New York State Historical Association, Smith-Telfer Collection, Cooperstown, NY
Back Cover: Jim Battles/DPA (woodpecker); Jonathan Wallen (rhododendron); Paul Rezendes (woodchuck)